2003

To Lynn,

Happy Holidays.

Enjoy my culinary road trip

Mary Ellen Winston

THE NEW YORK CABBIE COOKBOOK

Appetizers and First Courses Meat and Poultry Fish and Seafood Hearty Soups and Stews Casseroles and Skillet Meals Side Dishes and Salads Breads and Baked Goods Desserts and Other Sweet Things Appetizers and First Courses Meat and Poultry Fish and Seafood Hearty Soups and Stews Casseroles and Skillet Meals Side Dishes and Salads Breads and Baked Goods Desserts and Other Sweet Things Appetizers and First Courses Meat and Poultry Fish and Seafood Hearty Soups and Stews Casseroles and Skillet Meals Side Dishes and Salads Breads and Baked Goods Desserts and Other Sweet Things Appetizers and First Courses Meat and Poultry Fish and Seafood Hearty Soups and Stews Casseroles and Skillet Meals Side Dishes and Salads Breads and Baked Goods Desserts Other Sweet Things Appetizers and First Courses Meat and Poultry Fish and Seafood Hearty Soups and Stews Casseroles and Skillet Meals Side Dishes and Salads Breads and Baked Goods Desserts and Other Sweet Things Appetizers and First Courses Meat and Poultry Fish and Seafood Hearty Soups and Stews Casseroles and Skillet Meals Side Dishes and Salads Breads and Baked Goods Desserts and Other Sweet Things Appetizers and First Courses Meat and Poultry Fish and Seafood Hearty Soups and Stews Casseroles and Skillet Meals Side Dishes and Salads Breads and Baked Goods Desserts and Other Sweet Things Appetizers and First Courses Meat and Poultry Fish and Seafood Hearty Soups and Stews Casseroles and Skillet Meals Side Dishes and Salads Breads and Baked Goods Desserts and Other Sweet Things Appetizers and First Courses Meat and Poultry Fish and Seafood Hearty Soups and Stews Casseroles and Skillet Meals Side Dishes and Salads Breads and Baked Goods Desserts and Other Sweet Things Appetizers and First Courses Meat and Poultry Fish and Seafood Hearty Soups and Stews Casseroles and Skillet Meals Side Dishes and Salads Breads and Baked Goods Desserts and Other Sweet Things Appetizers and First Courses Meat and Poultry Fish and Seafood Hearty Soups and Stews Casseroles and Skillet Meals Side Dishes Salads Breads and Baked Goods Desserts and Other Sweet Things Appetizers and First Courses Meat and Poultry Fish and Seafood Hearty Soups and Stews Casseroles and Skillet Meals Side Dishes and Salads Breads and Baked Goods Desserts and Other Sweet Things Appetizers and First Courses Meat and Poultry Fish and Seafood Hearty Soups and Stews Casseroles and Skillet Meals Side Dishes and Salads Breads and Baked Goods Desserts and Other Sweet Things Appetizers and First Courses Meat and Poultry Fish and Seafood Hearty Soups and Stews Casseroles and Skillet Meals Side Dishes and Salads Breads and Baked Goods Desserts and Other Sweet Things Appetizers and First Courses Meat and Poultry Fish and Seafood Hearty Soups and Stews Casseroles Skillet Meals Side Dishes and Salads Breads and Baked Goods Desserts and Other Sweet Things

THE NEW YORK CABBIE COOKBOOK

MORE THAN 120
AUTHENTIC HOMESTYLE RECIPES FROM
AROUND THE GLOBE

BY MARY ELLEN WINSTON AND HOLLY GARRISON

RUNNING PRESS
PHILADELPHIA · LONDON

9   8   7   6   5   4   3   2   1
Digit on the right indicates the number of this printing

Library of Congress Control Number: 2002109122

ISBN 0-7624-1228-3

Cover design and interior design by Frances J. Soo Ping Chow
Edited by Justin Schwartz
Typography: Antique Olive, BundesbahnPI,
and Memphis

This book may be ordered by mail from the publisher.
Please include $2.50 for postage and handling.
But try your bookstore first!

Running Press Book Publishers
125 South Twenty-second Street
Philadelphia, Pennsylvania 19103-4399

Visit us on the web!
www.runningpress.com

Contents

I dedicate this book to my sons Michael and David

who grew up in spite of my cooking.

They would say, "Mom, this is really good . . . what is it?"

They called me The Mystery Chef.

—Mary Ellen Winston

How This Cookbook Happened

FOR MORE THAN THIRTY YEARS I've worked as a costume designer in movies, television, and the theater. In short, that means I'm responsible for conceiving and designing "the look" of the wardrobe, and am charged with obtaining what every cast member wears, from top hat and tails to Neanderthal loin cloths.

In my line of work, travel can sometimes mean exotic locations, but more often than not, my destination is more like a lower-Manhattan warehouse stuffed with vintage clothing, or a manufacturer in the South Bronx who still makes a certain pearled button, or a Seventh Avenue trimming shop that carries a rare lace that I need for an eighteenth-century epic film. Fortunately, there is very little that can't be rented, bought, or borrowed in "The Big Apple."

The pace is frenzied, and some days I feel more pressured than a futures trader: rush, rush, rush; hurry, hurry, hurry; time is money. "Versace is *not* in this budget. Find a knock-off that works!" "Why couldn't it be here today?" "We really needed that yesterday." Most of the time, I can do it, thanks to countless New York City cab drivers, who have been my salvation. Cabbies are the ones who have helped me to accomplish my often unrealistic expectations. But more than that, they've helped

me to hang on to my mental health. I think my state of desperation must have rubbed off on many of them, when I'd frantically jump into a cab (as many as eight or ten a day) and try to explain in one quick sentence how late I was and what still had to be done in an impossibly short amount of time.

In my hours spent in cabs, I have become ever more aware of the thread that binds me to these new Americans. They are following a path once taken by my own forebears. Cab drivers are part of a new wave of immigrants to the United States. Many are from the Middle East and less developed countries, and they always make me think of my grandfather, who came to the United States from Russia in 1876.

My grandfather worked hard. He traveled from town to town in Ohio in a horse-drawn buggy, selling pots, pans, and yard goods. With every few extra dollars he made, Grandfather would send for yet another relative to come to America, much the same as cab drivers do today.

My en route discourses with my drivers were once basic—friendly, distracting chats prompted by Polaroids of children clipped to the visor, or a name on a license that immediately identified my driver as being from a particular country of interest.

Eventually, these conversations led me to this book, for it is food, I discovered, that is the greatest common denominator of an extremely diverse and often divided world.

One miserable day, while working in a snowstorm, I hailed a cab with an Indian driver who was willing to stay with me all day. My mission that day was to replace eight costumes for a last-minute cast change on a major television show. In my usual haste, I hadn't given thought to eating, but as the day wore on and I was stuffing the trunk and even the front seat with wardrobe, my famished driver offered to take us to a little Indian restaurant nearby where he chose lunch for both of us. It was a real movable feast that included chicken *masala*, rice *pulao*, *raita*, and *naan*, which we literally ate on the run. As we munched along during the ride, he explained to me the sharp differences between a *vindaloo* and a *masala*, ticked off twenty varieties of Indian bread, and straightened me out about the endless varieties of curry. Although the dishes we ate that day were wonderful, none of them, he said, were as good as those his mother made back in India.

I think it was lunch that day that planted the seed for this cookbook. As a passionate food lover, I became ever more intrigued with what my drivers told me—with very little encouragement, I should add—about their native cuisines. They were not only willing, but very anxious to share their culinary knowledge. Many drivers extended invitations for me to come to their homes so that I could sample their food. Others gave me recipes for old-country favorites that their wives, husbands, mothers, and grandmothers cooked for them. The light finally snapped on, and *The New York Cabbie Cookbook* came to life. What better tribute to those dedicated and good-natured drivers, as well as to my own, very special hometown?

For more than a year I gathered recipes and information about the drivers who gave them to me. I even went so far as to invade taxi garages. I worked the cab lines, rapping on driver-side windows like some crazed political candidate. Amazingly, after I explained what I needed and why, most cabbies would be in touch within a day or two to make arrangements to mail or drop off a recipe or two at my apartment house. I never expected such enthusiasm, and it was infectious.

Looking back, I feel so very fortunate and grateful to have had cabbies who would gently suggest that I catch my breath, calm down, try not to worry, and then do their best to help me meet and often beat my impossible deadlines.

My hope is that, through this book, these New York cabbies can do for you what they did for me. Besides providing recipes for some excellent eating, they awoke in me a dormant sense of humility and gratitude, until one day I recognized and acknowledged that I really do have quite a wonderful life in this greatest of all cities.

—MARY ELLEN WINSTON

TAXICABS ARE A VITAL and intrinsic part of New York City's vast transportation system, and very much like the city itself in the freedom that they offer. Hail one of these popular forms of public conveyance at any time of the day or night, on any street corner or curbside, and you can go almost anywhere, get just about anything, and not have to think about astronomical parking rates, car theft, or any one of the other worries that accompany auto ownership in a town where a car can be far more frustrating than convenient.

It's interesting, when you think about it, the way we routinely leap into cabs, entrusting our very lives to the drivers' skills and their knowledge of the city's landscape to get us where we're going as quickly as possible.

The men and women who drive cabs are also amazingly like New York. They can be funny, charming, exhilarating, unfailingly unflappable, and sometimes frustrating, but ultimately they are so diverse that they simply can't be pigeonholed in any way. The single thing that

Profile in Gratitude
Cabbie: **Sam Goldstein**
Country of Origin: Germany

"The best tip I ever got was a long time ago from Marilyn Monroe. She kissed me," says Sam, an eighty-something-year-old cab driver who came to New York soon after being liberated from a German concentration camp in 1945. He says now that he liked "the style," as he calls it, of the American GI's who freed him so much that he immediately went to the United Jewish Appeal and asked to be relocated to the United States.

"Another time," he recalls, "I picked up George Hamilton and told him to be more careful. He was standing in the middle of the street." To which Hamilton replied, "I wish my wife cared as much about me as you seem to." Janet Leigh was another famous backseat personality. The two connected immediately when Sam mentioned that his wife and Leigh's then-husband Bernie Schwartz (better known as Tony Curtis) went to school together.

Celebrities aside, Sam loves his passengers. In the nearly fifty years he's been driving, he has saved at least one man from certain death by rushing him to the nearest emergency room. A year later, he picked up the same man, who recognized him and offered a belated fifty-dollar tip. Sam declined, just as he declined having the baby named after him, who came frighteningly close to being born in Sam's cab during a fast ride to the hospital.

"I have always loved the United States and New York," Sam says in a wistful voice. "Even though I have been a citizen here for many years, I pray that I will never take this beautiful country for granted and say bad things about it, like some people who were born here do. I try to tell them how lucky they are. I hope they listen to me."

cabbies do have in common is that all forty thousand or so of them are unofficial New York City ambassadors, and are frequently the first and last people tourists and visitors encounter on their way in and out of the city. By virtue of this alone they can set the tone for the New York experience or memory.

Old-Time Cabbies

Time was when driving a taxicab was a lifetime profession, and the cabbies were easily defined caricatures of themselves. During those simpler times cabbies were almost always New Yorkers by birth, or at least by long advocacy. Each man (there were no women drivers until relatively recently) knew and loved the city nearly as well as his own home or apartment,

which was usually in Brooklyn, the Bronx, or Queens, and the cab itself functioned as the family car on Sunday afternoons. But like the legendary Checker cabs they often drove, these cabbies have all but disappeared into history.

New-Wave Cabbies

New Yorkers grumble about the demise in the art of cab driving, but they are also quick to accept anything new, and they readily concede that the new crop of drivers—those who have come to New York City from such disparate places as Pakistan, Russia, and West Africa—have something just as important to offer.

These cabbies have stories to tell about the places they were born and raised, and offer insightful thoughts that

Profile in Gratitude

Cabbie: **Grame Traore**

Country of Origin: Mali, West Africa

"I have been in the United States for nine years. My wife, Niakale, came four years ago. We are both well educated with bachelors' degrees in biology. I also have two years' studies in economic sciences from the National School of Administration of Bamako, and my wife finished her studies at the National School of Post and Telecommunication in Bamako before coming to New York to be together.

"We came here with a hope to continue our education. My wish is to become a medical doctor, perhaps in research. In this land of many opportunities, since this first step of coming here is done, we are full of hope for a better life filled with happiness.

"Niakale and I now have two beautiful children, who were born here, a girl first and then a boy. Most of all we want our children to grow up in this country, where they can receive a good education for their future life.

"Will all of this happen like we expect it? We don't know, but we will try our best for it."

can't be found in a book or on a map. They can tell you how life *really* is in the country they left, and how they perceive its economics, social structure, and customs in ways that make newspaper headlines more personal, vivid, and compelling. To become acquainted with many of New York City's cab drivers, even briefly, is in a very real sense to become better acquainted with the world.

Cabbies are also amazingly well informed about local and national news, many of them much more so than the American-born passengers they carry. As one cabbie so aptly put it: "Where I come from there is no newspaper, at least none that can be believed. Although I am here for many years and am a citizen for a long time, I still can't believe how newspapers give me the news, even if it is to say bad things about our country and our leaders. I read two New York papers from front to back every day. This also gives me prac-

tice in mastering my new language and teaches me different words."

Stepping Stone to a New Life

Cab drivers nowadays generally view their job as merely a stepping stone toward an ultimately better life, and they frequently lead dual and difficult lives in order to get there. When they aren't driving (often for as many as twelve hours a day), they are pursuing careers, working at other jobs, and going to school. So intense was the desire of these people to emigrate to the United States that many left good jobs, careers, and professions to do it. As we pay our fares, most of us can't help but be amazed that we live in a country that still compels people to leave families, common interests, local surroundings, and seemingly lucrative occupations to come here and drive a cab.

Chapter 1 Appetizers and First Courses Meat and Poultry Fish and Seafood Hearty Soups and Stews Casseroles and Skillet Meals Side Dishes and Salads Breads and Baked Goods Desserts and Other Sweet Things Appetizers and First Courses Meat and Poultry Fish and Seafood Hearty Soups and Stews Casseroles and Skillet Meals Side Dishes and Salads Breads and Baked Goods Desserts Other Sweet Things Appetizers and First Courses Meat and Poultry Fish and Seafood Hearty Soups and Stews Casseroles and Skillet Meals Side Dishes and Salads Breads and Baked Goods Desserts and Other Sweet Things Appetizers and First Courses Meat and Poultry Fish and Seafood Hearty Soups and Stews Casseroles and Skillet Meals Side Dishes and Salads Breads and Baked Goods Desserts and Other Sweet Things Appetizers and First Courses Meat and Poultry Fish and Seafood Hearty Soups and Stews Casseroles and Skillet Meals Side Dishes and Salads Breads and Baked Goods Desserts and Other Sweet Things Appetizers and First Courses Meat and Poultry Fish and Seafood Hearty Soups and Stews Casseroles and Skillet Meals Side Dishes and Salads Breads Baked Goods Desserts and Other Sweet Things **Appetizers and First Courses** Meat and Poultry Fish and Seafood Hearty Soups and Stews Casseroles and Skillet Meals Side Dishes and Salads Breads Baked Goods Desserts and Other Sweet Things Appetizers and First Courses Meat and Poultry Fish and Seafood Hearty Soups and Stews Casseroles and Skillet Meals Side Dishes and Salads Breads Baked Goods Desserts and Other Sweet Things Appetizers and First Courses Meat and Poultry Fish and Seafood Hearty Soups and Stews Casseroles and Skillet Meals Side Dishes and Salads Breads and Baked Goods Desserts and Other Sweet Things Appetizers and First Courses Meat and Poultry Fish and Seafood Hearty Soups and Stews Casseroles and Skillet Meals Side Dishes and Salads Breads and Baked Goods Desserts and Other Sweet Things Appetizers and First Courses Meat and Poultry Fish and Seafood Hearty Soups and Stews Casseroles and Skillet Meals Side Dishes and Salads Breads and Baked Goods Desserts and Other Sweet Things Appetizers and First Courses Meat and Poultry Fish and Seafood Hearty Soups and Stews Casseroles and Skillet Meals Side Dishes and Salads Breads and Baked Goods Desserts and Other Sweet Things Appetizers and First Courses Meat and Poultry Fish and Seafood Hearty Soups and Stews Casseroles and Skillet Meals Side Dishes and Salads Breads and Baked Goods Desserts and Other Sweet Things Appetizers and First Courses Meat and Poultry Fish and Seafood Hearty Soups and Stews Casseroles and Skillet Meals Side Dishes and Salads Breads and Baked Goods Desserts and Other Sweet Things Appetizers and First Courses Meat and Poultry Fish and Seafood Hearty Soups and Stews Casseroles and Skillet Meals Side Dishes and Salads Breads and Baked Goods Desserts and Other Sweet Things

TAXI TRIVIA: In 1969, yellow became the standard color for all New York City licensed cabs in order to distinguish them from "gypsy" cabs.

Cabbie: **Igor Pronine**

Country of Origin: Russia

PROFILE: "Since I was a boy, I want to visit America, but I never dreamed I would live here. America was legend. My grandfather showed me pictures of the Statue of Liberty and big buildings in New York. I never forgot that. Even today, when I am driving downtown, I must always look at the lady statue to believe I am really in this country."

BEING A CABBIE: "It's a good living for now. I know my way around New York better than most people born here. I never get lost and I never have bad things happen to me."

MOST MEMORABLE FARES: "Harrison Ford. He was polite, not much to say. A good tip he gives me, but not too much. When I tell my wife, she was very sad I did not ask him to sign his name."

ABOUT NEW YORK/AMERICA: "What do I like most about America? Freedom. I love America, and I think it must be hard for Americans to know what it is like not to live free. Things were very hard for us in Russia. It takes time, I think, to know how to be free."

"Vindgret"

Elena's Vegetable, Apple, and Sauerkraut Salad

An unusual combination of root vegetables and apples, this salad's unique character is provided by the tangy taste of sauerkraut, dill pickle, and a touch of sugar, ingredients a Russian family is always likely to have on hand. Igor's wife, Elena, says that occasionally *vindgret* is eaten with herring, but more commonly with bread or crackers, along with small chunks of a pungent grating cheese, such as thin slivers of medium-aged Asiago, which most closely resembles the cheese used in Russia.

MAKES 8 TO 12 APPETIZER SERVINGS

3 small beets, rinsed, leaf stems and roots left intact

3 or 4 boiling potatoes, peeled and cut into ½-inch cubes (about 2 cups)

1 or 2 carrots, trimmed, scraped, and cut into ½-inch cubes (about 1 cup)

1 firm, tart apple, peeled, cored, and cut into small cubes (1¼ to 1½ cups)

½ cup finely chopped dill pickle

1 (8-ounce) can sauerkraut, drained and rinsed

6 tablespoons olive or vegetable oil

2 tablespoons white vinegar

1 teaspoon sugar

⅛ teaspoon salt

Freshly ground black pepper, to taste

Caraway seeds, to taste (optional)

1 In a medium-size saucepan, boil the beets in water to cover until fork-tender, 35 to 40 minutes. Drain and rinse with cold water. When the beets are cool enough to handle, slip off the skins, trim the root and stem ends, then cut into small cubes.

2 Meanwhile, in a large saucepan, boil the cubed potatoes and carrots together in lightly salted water until both are fork-tender, about 5 minutes. Drain in a colander, then set aside in a large bowl. Add the beets, apple, pickle, and sauerkraut.

3 While the vegetables are cooking, in a small bowl, whisk together the oil, vinegar, sugar, salt, pepper, and caraway seeds, if using. Pour over the warm vegetables and toss gently until the mixture is evenly coated with dressing. Cover and refrigerate for 2 or 3 hours before serving. Cover and refrigerate leftovers, which will keep well for 1 to 2 days.

TAXI TRIVIA: The average price for a fleet cab medallion is about $250,000. The City first began to issue medallions, basically a license to do business, in the early 1900s. The number of medallions in New York City (fixed by law) is now 12,187. The purpose of the City-issued medallions is to control the number of cabs, thus guaranteeing each cab owner a profitable business. The medallion offers the passenger a guarantee as well. Among other things, it assures the rider that the cab is well maintained, properly insured, and reasonably clean, and that the driver is sober, honest, and reliable.

Cabbie: **Rivka Moskovich**

Country of Origin: Israel

Other Recipes:

Chicken Baked with Oranges (see page 64)

Meat-and-Tomato-Stuffed Eggplant (see page 121)

Glazed Oranges with Mint Syrup (see page 179)

PROFILE: "I came here from Tel Aviv in 1973 to work in the diamond trade, and I guess you could say I was pretty well off when I got here, so I bought a cab as an investment. A few years ago, when the diamond business went bad for a while, I ended up driving it."

BEING A CABBIE: "On my first day out I was terrified. I didn't know what to do or where to go, but I survived, and everything got better." When asked if any customers have ever run off without paying the fare, she said, "Of course . . . regular stuff."

MEMORABLE FARES: Anthony Hopkins, who told her not to miss *The Merchant of Venice* with Dustin Hoffman. She did go. "He was right. It was wonderful."

ABOUT NEW YORK/AMERICA: "New York is one of the most interesting places in the world, where there is good food, good art, and good music. I love it."

Roasted Eggplant Salad

Even if you are not a big fan of eggplant, Rivka urges you to try roasting it, and you may change your mind. "This is especially true when the eggplant is roasted on a charcoal grill, and the smoky flavor is absorbed into the flesh," she says. This versatile salad can be served as an appetizer, a first course, or even a side dish. When serving it as an appetizer spread, accompany it with lightly toasted, very thinly sliced rounds of a baguette.

MAKES 4 TO 6 APPETIZER SERVINGS

2 medium-size eggplants
  (each weighing 1¼ to 1½ pounds)
3 tablespoons extra-virgin olive oil
2 tablespoons freshly squeezed lemon juice
1 large clove garlic, puréed (see Note)
½ to ¾ teaspoon salt
⅛ teaspoon freshly ground black pepper

1 Position a rack in the center of the oven. Preheat the oven broiler. With the tip of a knife, puncture the eggplants several times on all sides to prevent their exploding in the oven. Place the eggplants directly on the oven rack, 6 to 8 inches below the source of heat. (The eggplants for this salad can also be roasted on a charcoal grill, 3 or 4 inches above medium-hot coals.) Roast, turning occasionally, until the eggplants are well charred, 30 to 40 minutes. They should be very soft and just starting to collapse. (There will be some smoking and sizzling, but this is to be expected.) Remove the eggplants from the oven, and transfer to a platter. While they are still hot, strip off the skin, which will come away very easily with the help of a knife tip. Set the peeled eggplants, stem-side up, in a colander set over a bowl. Cover the eggplant in the colander snugly with plastic wrap and refrigerate for several hours, or overnight, to drain.

2 When ready to make the salad, remove the eggplants from the colander to a work surface. Cut off the end of each eggplant about 1 inch below the stem. Split the eggplants open lengthwise. Carefully remove the strips of seeds, scraping them off the flesh with the tip of a spoon. (It won't be pos-sible to get them all, but this step is impor-tant, since it's the seeds that tend to make eggplant bitter.) Chop the eggplants very finely, and place in a medium-size bowl.

3 To make the dressing, in a small bowl, whisk together the olive oil, lemon juice, garlic purée, salt, and pepper. Stir the dressing into the chopped eggplant until well combined. Use a dinner fork to break up any large lumps of eggplant, mashing them against the side of the bowl. Transfer the eggplant mixture to a serving bowl. Cover and chill for several hours to give the flavors time to blend. Bring to room temperature before serving.

NOTE: How to Purée Garlic—After the garlic has been peeled, use a knife to mince it as finely as possible. Sprinkle the minced garlic with a very small amount of kosher salt (the rough edges of these coarse salt crystals help to break down the garlic) and mash with the back of a dinner fork until the garlic is smooth.

BIG APPLE BITE: In 1698, 4,937 people lived in New York City.

Today, that many people work in an average-sized Midtown office building.

Cabbie: **Yazid Anes**
Country of Origin: Algeria

Other Recipes:

Checkouka: A Skillet Meal of Eggs, Roasted Peppers, and Tomatoes (see page 132)

Carrot Salad (see page 160)

Roasted Peppers with Vinaigrette

"In Algeria, this salad is often served on toasted bread that is very much like a toasted English muffin," says Yazid. "Sometimes for lunch I bring along a sandwich that I make with pepper strips and some vinegar dressing on a hard roll." As an afterthought, he adds: "I do not mean to sound condescending, but in Algeria there is a strong French influence on our cooking, which I think makes it better than some of the food in this part of the world."

Roasting bell peppers (red, green, yellow, purple, or whatever color they may be) gives the peppers a whole new dimension of softness, sweetness, and intensity of flavor. The peppers can be served plain with just a touch of extra-virgin olive oil and a few drops of balsamic or red wine vinegar. They can also be embellished with such things as tiny black olives, crumbled goat or feta cheese, or merely chopped fresh basil or thinly sliced scallions. Roasted peppers are a delicious addition to an antipasti plate, along with such tasty tidbits as Stuffed Grape Leaves (see page 20), chunks of cheese, sliced hard sausage, and even a few steamed shrimp.

MAKES 4 TO 6 APPETIZER SERVINGS

3 large red bell peppers
3 large green bell peppers
¼ cup Basic Vinaigrette (recipe follows)

1 Preheat the oven broiler. Have ready a baking sheet lined with aluminum foil. Cut the stem out of the top of each pepper, then cut off about ¼ inch from the tops and bottoms. With your fingers, pull out the seed cores. Cut down one side of each pepper, then spread it out on a work surface, skin-side down. With a knife, trim away the white ribs and flick away any stray seeds. Arrange the peppers (including the tops and bottoms, if you like), skin-side up on the prepared baking sheet, flattening each piece as much as possible with the palm of your hand.

2 Slide the baking sheet beneath the broiler and broil until the skins are evenly and well charred (blackened) but the peppers are still fairly firm, about 6 minutes. Remove the baking sheet from the oven, and immediately cover the baking pan tightly with another piece of foil to create steam while the peppers are cooling. When the peppers are cool, peel and rub away the skin, which will come off easily in large pieces.

3 Cut the peppers crosswise into ¼-inch strips. Place the roasted peppers in a salad dish and toss with the vinaigrette.

Basic Vinaigrette

MAKES ABOUT ½ CUP

1 small clove garlic, cut in half
2 tablespoons plus 2 teaspoons red wine vinegar
½ teaspoon Dijon mustard (optional)
1 teaspoon salt
½ teaspoon freshly ground black pepper
6 tablespoons extra-virgin olive oil

Rub the bottom of a small bowl with the cut sides of the garlic. Add the vinegar, mustard, salt, and pepper to the bowl, and whisk until well blended. Add the oil, and whisk for about 30 seconds, until the mixture is slightly thickened. Store in the refrigerator in a tightly covered container for no longer than a couple of days. Bring to room temperature and shake well before using.

BIG APPLE BITE: Broadway is actually one of the world's longest streets. Although widely known for housing some of the best theatrical works, the street goes a long way past the city lights, stretching 150 miles to Albany.

Cabbie: **Eman Abyseif**

Country of Origin: Egypt

Other Recipes:

Lentil Soup (see page 94)

Stuffed Grape Leaves

"If you can find a source for fresh grapevine leaves—smaller ones, preferably—by all means try them," says this cabbie. "But you must be sure that they are edible." (This means that they have not been treated with pesticides or other chemicals.) "Then the leaves must be soaked in boiling water, just like canned leaves, and you must also take the time to trim away the stem by snipping a little V in the bottom of the leaf if the canning factory has not already done this for you. In Egypt, of course, we never have to use canned leaves, which have a slightly tart and salty flavor, but here it is so hard to find fresh leaves that we have learned to adjust our taste to the canned."

The stuffed leaves can be served by themselves, usually with chunks of feta cheese, or as part of a large antipasti platter as suggested in the recipe for Roasted Peppers with Vinaigrette (see page 18).

MAKES 32 STUFFED LEAVES; 6 TO 8 APPETIZER SERVINGS

1 (16-ounce) jar or can grape leaves packed in vinegar brine (you will need 32 leaves)

3 tablespoons extra-virgin olive oil

1 medium-size yellow onion, shredded (about ½ cup)

1 clove garlic, minced

½ pound ground lamb

1 cup cooked brown rice (about ⅓ cup raw)

1 tablespoon chopped fresh dill

1 tablespoon finely chopped fresh mint

1 tablespoon minced fresh parsley

1 teaspoon salt

¼ teaspoon freshly ground black pepper

2 cups (16 ounces) chicken broth (see page 92)

Extra-virgin olive oil, for brushing

Very thin lemon slices and dill sprigs, for garnish

1 Carefully remove the grape leaves from the jar or can (they are packed in fat, cigar-like rolls), although they are sturdier than you might imagine. Unroll and separate the leaves and spread them in layers in a large, shallow pan. Add enough boiling water to cover the leaves generously. Set aside until the water has cooled. Rinse the leaves with cool water, drain well, and pat dry with paper towels. Set aside until ready to fill.

2 Heat 1 tablespoon of the oil in a large skillet over high heat. When it is hot, add the onion and garlic, and cook over medium heat, stirring, until the onion is tender, about 3 minutes. Add the ground lamb, and cook, stirring and breaking up the

meat with the side of a spoon, until it is completely crumbled and no pink remains. Off the heat, stir in the cooked rice, dill, mint, parsley, salt, and pepper until well blended. Set aside for about 30 minutes to cool.

3 Lay one grape leaf flat, vein-side up, and pointed end away from you, on a work surface. Place about 1 tablespoon (a little more or less, depending on the size of the leaf) of the meat mixture just below the center of each grape leaf. Fold the bottom of the leaf over the filling, fold the sides over the filling, then roll into a small, oblong package. Do not fold too tightly. Leave just a little room for any expansion that may take place during cooking. (Because the leaves vary in size, some packets will be larger or smaller than others.) Repeat this procedure with the remaining grape leaves and filling. As the leaves are stuffed, arrange them smooth-side up in the bottom of a large, heavy saucepan, fitting the leaf packets together tightly.

4 Pour the chicken broth mixed with the remaining 2 tablespoons of the olive oil over the packets so that they are just barely covered, adding a little water, if necessary. Cook over medium-low heat at a very slow simmer for 45 minutes. (If the liquid is allowed to simmer too rapidly, it may dislodge the leaf packets and cause them to come apart.) Set the pot aside until cool, then carefully remove the stuffed leaves from the pot to a shallow dish. Brush them with extra-virgin olive oil to keep them from drying out. Cover and refrigerate if not serving the day they are made.

5 The stuffed leaves can be served warm or at room temperature. If serving warm, the easiest way to reheat the packets is to leave them in the cooking pan and rewarm over very low heat. If serving at room temperature, set out for about 1 hour before serving. The stuffed leaves will keep well in the refrigerator for several days.

6 To serve, arrange the leaves on a serving platter, and garnish with lemon slices and dill sprigs.

BIG APPLE BITE: In Times Square, as many as 8,500 pedestrians will pass a given spot per hour—that's two-and-a-half people per second.

Cabbie: **Victor Babicz**

Country of Origin: Argentina

Other Recipes:

Chimichurri: Steak with Parsley and Garlic Sauce (see page 40)

"Madambre"

Steak Roll Stuffed with Diced Vegetable Salad

"In my family we slice the roll thinly and eat it as an appetizer," says Victor, "although Americans, who don't eat as much meat as we do, might prefer to serve the *madambre* as part of a table of cold foods, or for a picnic. Any way you eat it, this roll is delicious. To drink? That's easy. We drink espresso with almost everything!" Victor serves his cold Diced Vegetable Salad as an accompaniment to the meat. "It's almost like a thick dressing, which is spooned over and eaten with the meat," he says.

Preparation for this recipe must be started the day before serving.

MAKES 12 TO 16 APPETIZER SERVINGS

1 beef flank steak (about 1¾ pounds)

Salt and freshly ground black pepper, to taste

1 bunch fresh parsley, minced (about 1 cup)

4 slender scallions, including most of the green tops, trimmed

2 slender carrots, peeled and trimmed

1 red bell pepper, cored, seeded, and cut into thin strips

3 hard-cooked eggs, peeled and cut in half lengthwise

3 cups beef broth (see page 92)

Diced Vegetable Salad

1 boiling potato, peeled and cut into ½-inch cubes (about 1 cup)

1 or 2 carrots, peeled, trimmed, and cut into ½-inch cubes (about 1 cup)

1 cup fresh or frozen peas

1 (8¼-ounce) can whole or sliced beets, drained, rinsed, and cut into small cubes

Salt and freshly ground black pepper, to taste

Mayonnaise

1 With the short end facing you, lay the flank steak on a work surface, sinewy-side down, and pound it with a rolling pin or some other heavy, smooth object until it measures about 12 x 8 inches. Season with salt and pepper, then sprinkle evenly with the parsley. Arrange the scallions, carrots, and pepper strips across the meat, leaving about 1 inch at the top and bottom of the meat. Arrange the eggs in three evenly spaced rows over the vegetables across the center of the meat. Season with salt and pepper again. Carefully roll up the meat, keeping everything in place as much as possible. (You may need another pair of hands to help accomplish this.) With a piece of kitchen string, tie the roll around in several places; also tie the roll lengthwise. Cut a 24-inch, triple-thick length of cheesecloth. Lay the meat roll on one end of the cheesecloth and roll it up firmly, then tie the ends of the cheesecloth tightly with string.

2 Place the roll in a heavy saucepan that is just large enough to hold it comfortably. Add the beef broth, then add just enough water so that the liquid barely covers the roll. Bring to a fast simmer, then lower the heat so that the broth simmers slowly. Cover and cook for 2 hours. Remove the pan from the heat, and set aside to cool for about 1 hour. Remove the meat roll from the broth to a platter. Cover, and refrigerate for about 24 hours. Reserve and refrigerate about ½ cup of the broth. Freeze or refrigerate the remaining broth to use for other purposes.

3 Prepare the Diced Vegetable Salad: In a medium-size saucepan, add the potato and carrot with enough lightly salted water to cover, and bring to a boil. Reduce the heat, cover, and simmer until the vegetables are barely tender, about 5 minutes. Add the peas, and cook for 1 minute longer. Drain the vegetables into a colander, and set aside until slightly cooled.

4 Transfer the vegetables to a medium-size bowl. Add the beets, and toss until combined. Season with salt and pepper. Gradually add mayonnaise to taste, and stir gently until well combined. The mixture should be fairly moist. Cover, and refrigerate until ready to serve, or for at least 1 hour.

5 When ready to serve, unwrap and untie the meat. With a long, very sharp knife, cut the roll into thin slices, and serve with the Diced Vegetable Salad.

TAXI TRIVIA: Most New York cabs are Ford Crown Victorias that are specially built to withstand the rigors of cab service, in what is called the "police package." This model features, among other things, a heavy-duty transmission, shock absorbers, battery, and cooling system. In 2001, the NYC Taxi & Limousine Commission approved the Ford "Stretch" Crown Victoria, which features six extra inches of passenger leg room.

Cabbie: **Jose Molina**
Country of Origin: Ecuador

Shrimp Ceviche

"Most Americans have weak tongues," says Jose Molina, who likes to add an incendiary touch to his ceviche by including one small stemmed, seeded, and finely chopped serrano chile (be sure to wash your hands thoroughly afterward) in the marinade. *Ceviche* (pronounced seh-VEE-chay and sometimes spelled with an "s") is traditionally made with raw fish or shrimp that are "cooked" in an acidic juice. For those who are squeamish about eating raw seafood, these briefly cooked shrimp are a good alternative, and "briefly" is the key word here. If the shrimp are cooked too long, they become rubbery. If you're in a real rush, substitute about ¾ pound of cooked, peeled shrimp, but the flavor of the marinade will not be as pronounced. Ceviche can be served as a predinner bite with cocktails. Provide toothpicks to spear the shrimp, and plenty of napkins. Or arrange the shrimp on lettuce with thin slices of avocado, and serve as a first course or light luncheon or supper dish. "I like to drink pilsner beer with ceviche," says this cabbie cook.

MAKES 6 APPETIZER SERVINGS

1 large red onion, cut in half through the stem and the halves cut into very thin vertical slices (about 2 cups)

½ cup freshly squeezed lime juice (3 or 4 limes)

3 tablespoons extra-virgin olive oil

Freshly ground black pepper, to taste

1 small red bell pepper, finely chopped (about ½ cup)

2 (8-ounce) bottles clam juice

2 cups water

1 pound medium-size shrimp (30 to 40 count), peeled and deveined

1 Place the onion slices in a small bowl. Add enough boiling water to cover them, and let stand for 5 minutes. Drain in a colander, and rinse with cold water; set aside.

2 In a serving bowl, whisk together the lime juice, olive oil, and black pepper. Stir in the chopped bell pepper and onion slices, and set aside.

3 In a large saucepan, bring the clam juice and water to a boil. Remove the pan from the heat. Add the shrimp to the boiling-hot juice mixture and leave for exactly 1 minute, at which point the shrimp will be pink and barely firm. Drain the shrimp well in a colander, then add them to the bowl containing the marinade. Toss until the shrimp are well coated. Cover, and refrigerate for several hours before serving.

Cabbie: **Wilson Eng**
Country of Origin: China

Other Recipes:
Fried Rice with Egg (see page 131)

"Jing-Sting Ho"
Steamed Oysters with Garlic-and-Ginger Sauce

"While you are in New York, you should take a taxi to Chinatown and go to a dim sum restaurant," advises Wilson. *Dim sum* are the Chinese words for "heart's desire," which certainly does describe these appetizer-size treats. Early in the day (at least before noon) is the best time to visit a dim sum restaurant, where you will usually find yourself seated at a big, round table, often with a large Chinese family, who will treat you with extreme courtesy, and where you will have great fun watching Chinese toddlers handling chopsticks. You don't order from a menu in an authentic dim sum restaurant. Instead, the staff continuously comes through the dining room carrying trays or wheeling carts that are filled with a variety of freshly made dim sum. You merely point to those things that appeal to you, which are then served on little plates. This goes on and on until you have finally had enough. The check is figured by merely counting the number of plates at your place.

Garlic-and-Ginger Sauce is also excellent for dipping steamed clams or shrimp, or fried or steamed dumplings. With these oysters Wilson recommends drinking ginseng tea, which most Asians credit with great restorative and curative powers.

MAKES 4 APPETIZER SERVINGS

16 large oysters in the shell, scrubbed and rinsed	2 tablespoons rice wine vinegar
¼ cup peanut oil	3 scallions, including a small portion of the green
2 cloves garlic, minced	tops, minced
1-inch piece fresh ginger, peeled and minced	
2 tablespoons light soy sauce	

1 Arrange the oysters in a single layer in the bottom of a roasting pan. Add about 2 cups of water and cover the pan tightly with aluminum foil. Set the pan over two stovetop burners. Cook over high heat, steaming the oysters just until they open slightly, about 10 minutes. (Discard any oysters that do not open.)

2 While the oysters are steaming, in a small, heavy saucepan set over high heat, heat the oil until very hot, 1 to 2 minutes. Add the garlic and ginger, and cook, stirring constantly, until the garlic is lightly browned. Remove from the heat, and stir in the soy sauce and vinegar. (The mixture will separate.)

3 Uncover the steamed oysters and, when they are just cool enough to handle, pull off the top shell, leaving the oyster in the deeper half of the shell.

4 Arrange 4 oysters on each of 4 plates. Spoon a small amount of the hot-oil mixture over each oyster. (The oil mixture must be hot, so if it has cooled too much, reheat to nearly boiling.) Scatter the scallions over the oysters, and serve immediately.

Cabbie: **Henry Eng**
Country of Origin: Hong Kong

Steamed Shrimp Won Tons with Sesame-Soy Dipping Sauce

In Chinese, Henry told us, *won ton* means "cloud swallow." Shrimp is Henry's favorite filling mixture for won tons when he makes them at home, but he says that 8 ounces of ground pork can be substituted. The cooking method remains the same. Think of won tons as Asian ravioli, and the whole process of making them becomes less intimidating.

MAKES 28 TO 30 WON TONS;

8 TO 12 APPETIZER SERVINGS

Sesame-Soy Dipping Sauce
½ cup rice wine vinegar
2 tablespoons light soy sauce
4 teaspoons sugar
⅔ cup water
2 teaspoons minced scallion greens
2 teaspoons sesame seeds,
  toasted (see Note)

Won Ton Filling
8 ounces medium-size shrimp (30 to 40 count),
  peeled, deveined, and finely chopped
  (about 1 cup, firmly packed)
4 canned water chestnuts, drained and minced
  (about ¼ cup)
1 tablespoon light soy sauce

2 teaspoons Chinese rice wine, or substitute
   dry sherry or vermouth

½ teaspoon salt

1 tablespoon peanut oil

1-inch piece fresh ginger, peeled and shredded
   (discard the stringy pieces that collect on the
   outside of the grater)

½ teaspoon cornstarch, dissolved in
   1½ teaspoons cold water

30 won ton wrappers

1 large egg, lightly beaten

1 Prepare the Sesame-Soy Dipping Sauce: In a small saucepan, combine the rice wine vinegar, soy sauce, sugar, and water. Bring the mixture to a boil over high heat. Remove the pan from the heat, and set aside to cool.

2 Prepare the Won Ton Filling: In a small bowl, stir together the shrimp, water chestnuts, soy sauce, sherry, and salt. (The recipe can be made ahead up to this point. Cover, and refrigerate for up to several hours.)

3 Heat the oil in a large skillet over medium-high heat. When the oil is very hot but not yet beginning to smoke, add the shrimp mixture and the ginger. Cook, stirring constantly for a few moments, until the shrimp are firm. Give the cornstarch mixture a stir to reblend it, then stir it into the shrimp mixture. Continue to stir until the liquid thickens. Immediately transfer the shrimp mixture to a bowl, and set aside for about 30 minutes to cool to room temperature.

4 Place a rounded measuring teaspoonful

of the filling in the center of each wrapper. With a fingertip, lightly smear the edges of the wrapper with the egg, then fold the wrapper over the filling to make a triangle. Pinch the edges together firmly. As each won ton is made, set it on a lightly oiled baking sheet and cover with a dry towel. Discard the remaining egg.

5 Lightly coat a collapsible steamer basket with cooking spray. To a large cooking pot, add enough water to come up to the bottom of the basket. Bring to a simmer over medium heat. Arrange as many won tons in the basket as will fit in one layer, leaving a little room for expansion between each one. Lower the basket into the pot. Increase the heat so that the water simmers briskly. Cover tightly and steam until the wrappers are soft and opaque and the filling is hot, 3 to 5 minutes. As the won tons are cooked, transfer them to a heatproof platter, cover with foil, and keep warm in a low (170°F) oven.

6 Just before serving, stir the scallion and toasted sesame seeds into the cooled Sesame-Soy Dipping Sauce. Serve the warm dumplings with the dipping sauce.

NOTE: To toast sesame seeds, scatter them in a small, cold skillet. Set the skillet over medium heat, and stir constantly just until the seeds begin to change color and smell very nutty. Remove from the heat, and continue to stir until cool.

Cabbie: **John Ferrari**

Country of Origin: United States

Creamed Scallops on Toast Points

John recommends serving these scallops as the first course for Christmas or other special-occasion dinner, as they do in his family. On Christmas, he and his brother share the cooking. "I do it one year, he does it the next." He explains that an Italian Christmas dinner is a multicourse affair. For the Ferraris, the meal usually begins with a calamari salad, followed by garlicky steamed mussels or these scallops in a creamy sauce. "And that's before we even get started on the pasta!"

To say that this is a very rich dish is an obvious understatement, but it is sumptuous, worth every calorie, and reminiscent of the food once served at the great old Continental restaurants that proliferated in New York back in the days when butter and cream were not a concern. However, the saving grace of this dish may be that the servings are small, and for any festive meal this may be a perfect first course.

MAKES 4 APPETIZER SERVINGS

4 slices thin-cut, home-style bread
24 bay scallops (about ¼ pound)
½ cup dry white wine or dry vermouth
½ cup heavy cream
4 tablespoons (½ stick) butter, cut into
  pieces and softened
⅛ teaspoon white pepper
Salt, to taste
Snipped chives, for garnish

1 To make toast points, trim the crusts from the bread, and cut into triangles. Arrange in a single layer on an ungreased baking sheet. Place under a preheated broiler and toast until golden on one side, watching carefully; turn and toast on the other side. Total toasting time will be no longer than 2 or 3 minutes.

2 Rinse the scallops and pat dry on paper towels. Pour the wine into a large, non-aluminum or non-iron skillet set over high heat. Bring to a boil and add the scallops. Immediately reduce the heat to a simmer, and cook the scallops, moving and turning them, just until they are firm and opaque, 2 to 3 minutes.

3 With a slotted spoon, remove the scallops from the skillet to a plate, and keep them warm. Raise the heat and add the cream to the skillet. Simmer briskly, stirring frequently, until large, lazy bubbles appear on the surface and the mixture has thickened enough to coat a spoon, about 5 minutes. Remove from the heat, and immediately stir in the butter, scallops, and white pepper. Continue to stir until the butter has blended into the cream. Season with salt.

4 Arrange two toast points on each of four plates. Divide the scallops and sauce evenly over the toast. Sprinkle with chives, and serve immediately.

VARIATION: For a colorful and tasty change, peel, seed, and finely chop a medium-size tomato and stir into the skillet just after it has been removed from the heat and before stirring in the butter, scallops, and white pepper.

Cabbie: **Georgia Georgafu**
Country of Origin: Greece

"Spanakopita"
Spinach Pie and a Greek Salad

Spanakopita is the famous spinach-and-phyllo pie that is served in Greek homes and Greek restaurants everywhere in the world. One piece is an excellent addition to an appetizer (*meze* plate), but the pie is also very satisfying when served along with Greek Salad for lunch or supper. By nature, Greek salads are rather casual arrangements of what's in season and what's on hand, with feta cheese, juicy Greek olives, and a lavish sprinkling of dried oregano mandatory. (Technically, in a so-called real Greek salad, lettuce is most noticeable by its absence, since the long, hot Greek summers render these tender greens long gone by the time cucumbers and tomatoes are ready.)

Georgia suggests drinking a dry white wine with this dish, or even icy-cold *retsina*, the mildly pine-scented and pine-flavored "wine of Greece."

MAKES 12 APPETIZER SERVINGS

---

2 (10-ounce) packages frozen chopped spinach, thawed and drained in a colander
½ cup extra-virgin olive oil
1 medium-size yellow onion, finely chopped (about ½ cup)
2 tablespoons chopped fresh dill
½ teaspoon salt
¼ teaspoon ground white pepper
2 large eggs, lightly beaten
1 cup small-curd cottage cheese
¾ cup crumbled feta cheese (4 ounces)

¼ pound (1 stick) butter, melted
1 (1-pound) package frozen phyllo dough, thawed as the package directs and brought to room temperature (see sidebar)
Greek Salad (recipe follows)

1 Press down on the thawed and drained spinach in the colander with your fist to remove as much of any remaining liquid as possible.

2 Heat 1 tablespoon of the oil in a large skillet set over medium-high heat. When the oil is hot, add the onion, and cook over medium heat, stirring frequently, until lightly browned. Stir in the spinach and the remaining olive oil, and continue to cook, stirring frequently, until the mixture stops steaming. (This can take as long as 15 minutes, depending on how much liquid is left in the spinach.) Stir in the dill, salt, and pepper until well blended. Turn the mixture into a large bowl, and refrigerate until cooled. Stir the eggs, cottage cheese, and feta cheese into the cooled spinach mixture until very well blended.

3 Position a rack in the center of the oven. Preheat the oven to 350°F. Use some of the melted butter to brush the bottom and sides of a 13 x 9-inch metal baking pan.

4 Remove the phyllo from the package to a work surface and smooth out the stack of sheets. You will need 8 sheets for this recipe, plus 2 or 3 more as insurance against tears and other little disasters.

5 Fold one sheet of the phyllo in half to make a double layer that is about the same size as the pan. Place the folded sheet of phyllo in the bottom of the prepared pan. Brush with melted butter. Add another 3 folded sheets of phyllo, brushing each with butter. Spoon the spinach filling over the phyllo layers, smoothing it out evenly with the back of a spoon. Add another 4 folded sheets of phyllo as before.

Brush the final sheet of phyllo with butter.

6 Using a pancake turner, go around all four sides of the pan, tucking the dough down neatly. With a long, sharp knife, cut the layers lengthwise into thirds. Then cut into diamond shapes.

7 Bake for 40 to 45 minutes, until the top is golden brown. Remove the pan to a wire rack to cool slightly before serving. Cover and refrigerate leftovers. To reheat, set the pan or individual pieces in a 300°F oven for 15 to 20 minutes, or until hot throughout, or microwave briefly at 50 percent power (although microwaving will soften the top layers of phyllo so that they will no longer be crisp and flaky).

Greek Salad

To construct a Greek salad, arrange a bed of bite-size pieces of romaine or iceberg lettuce leaves (about 1 cup per serving) on each plate. Garnish with cucumber slices, radish slices, cherry tomatoes or tomato quarters, small red onion rings or scallions, kalamata olives, crumbled feta cheese, and chopped anchovy fillets, the anchovies being reserved for those who like them. Sprinkle generously with dried oregano. Serve with a pepper grinder and cruets of extra-virgin olive oil and red wine vinegar, or wedges of lemon to be added or squeezed over the salad to each diner's taste.

HOW TO HANDLE PHYLLO DOUGH

Working with phyllo (*filo*)—ultrathin sheets of pastry dough, which dry out, split, shred, and crumble almost immediately when exposed to the air—can be a frustrating experience for American cooks. In Greece and Middle Eastern countries, where phyllo is a common ingredient, women begin mastering the art of making it from scratch at a tender age, and from then on it's practice, practice, practice.

These days packages of frozen phyllo are available at most supermarkets in the frozen foods section. Fresh phyllo, too, can often be found in Greek and Middle Eastern grocery stores, or it can be ordered by mail.

1 Thaw the package of frozen phyllo in the refrigerator for at least 8 hours or overnight, then slowly bring it to room temperature, which takes about 2 hours, before removing it from the box. Phyllo that has been stored in the refrigerator should also be brought to room temperature.

2 Remove the phyllo from the package, cut open the sealed bag containing the folded stack of dough sheets, and carefully unfold them on a smooth, dry surface. Immediately cover the stack with a piece of plastic wrap and then with a damp kitchen towel. (If a damp towel were placed directly on the dough, the sheets would immediately stick together.) Keep the stack covered as you work with it. Do not leave it uncovered for more than a minute or so.

3 Nearly all recipes using phyllo call for each sheet or a top sheet to immediately be brushed with melted butter (or other liquid fat) to keep it from disintegrating and to keep the sheets separate so that they will bake up into flaky layers. So have ready the melted butter and a pastry brush. When applying the butter, first brush the fragile edges of the dough—which are particularly liable to crack and crumble—and then work from the center out, brushing any wrinkles toward the outside edges.

AND A COUPLE OF CAVEATS

No matter how carefully phyllo is handled, you can almost count on tearing or otherwise destroying a sheet or two. Be prepared with a few extra sheets.

Unused phyllo can be tightly rewrapped and refrigerated but not frozen, which would make it brittle. Use refrigerated leftover phyllo as soon as possible. However, since most recipes call for a substantial number of phyllo sheets, most expert cooks would recommend that leftovers be discarded.

Cabbie: Steven Chan

Country of Origin: Hong Kong

Other Recipes:

Chinese Almond Cookies with Chinese Tea (see page 190)

Chinese Spareribs

"You may be surprised to learn that these ribs, which are a Chinese-restaurant favorite, are easy to make at home," says Steven. Although usually eaten as an appetizer, the ribs can be served as a main dish. In that case, Steven, who once worked as a cook in his family's Chinese restaurant, suggests accompaniments of Chinese noodles tossed with a little Asian sesame oil, along with a stir-fry of mixed vegetables or snow peas. Preparation for this recipe must be started at least 8 hours or the day before serving.

MAKES 6 TO 8 APPETIZER SERVINGS

2½ to 3 pounds pork spareribs
1 (7- to 8-ounce) jar hoisin sauce
3 cloves garlic, minced
½ cup water

1 With a sharp knife, cut the spareribs into individual ribs between the bones. To make the marinating sauce, in a large bowl, combine the hoisin sauce and garlic until blended. Swirl the water in the empty hoisin jar, then stir into the sauce mixture. Add the ribs, turning them until each one is well coated with the sauce. Cover the bowl, and refrigerate for at least 8 hours and for up to 24 hours.

2 Preheat the oven to 375°F. Arrange the ribs in a single layer on the rack of a broiler pan. Set the marinade aside. (This is a good time to use a couple of disposable aluminum roasting pans, since the sauce for the ribs makes an awful burned-on mess.) Bake, uncovered, for about 1 hour, turning the ribs and brushing with some of the reserved marinade every 15 minutes (but *not* during the last 15 minutes, since the sauce previously held raw meat), until the ribs are glazed and crisp at the edges. Serve warm or at room temperature.

TAXI TRIVIA: To make a good living, many cabbies drive ten to twelve hours a day.

Cabbie: **Jenail Singh**
Country of Origin: Pakistan

"Pakoras"
Fried Chickpea Dumplings

"We eat a lot of vegetarian meals in Pakistan," says Jenail, "and if you add a salad and a bowl of cut fresh fruit, these dumplings are filling enough to make a light, meatless meal for two persons." Americans, though, will probably find *pakoras* more useful as hors d'oeuvres, particularly if accompanied by a bowl of Ahmed Hassan's tangy Yogurt Sauce (see page 34) for dunking.

Chickpea flour, Jenail explains, is a fine powder made from milled, dried garbanzo beans that are also known as chickpeas. This flour is not difficult to find. Try Middle Eastern, Indian, or health-food stores.

Another unfamiliar ingredient, *garam masala*, an all-purpose spice blend (generally cardamom, cinnamon, cloves, coriander, cumin, and black pepper), instantly recognizable as the essential flavor in Pakistani and Indian cuisines, is carried by most specialty food stores and Middle Eastern markets.

MAKES 8 DUMPLINGS, OR 4 APPETIZER SERVINGS

1 cup chickpea flour
½ teaspoon baking powder
½ teaspoon salt
Big pinch cayenne pepper
¼ teaspoon garam masala
  (see headnote)
Vegetable oil, for frying
2 cups Yogurt Sauce (see page 34)

1 In a small bowl, whisk together the chickpea flour, baking powder, salt, cayenne, and garam masala until well blended. With a spoon, gradually beat in just enough water (about ½ cup) to form a thick batter. (It should be just firm enough to hold its shape.)

2 Meanwhile, in a deep, heavy, medium-size saucepan, heat about 3 inches of oil to a temperature of 375°F on a deep-fry thermometer.

3 Drop the batter by rounded measuring-tablespoonsful into the hot oil. Cook, turning the dumplings, until golden, about 3 minutes. With a slotted spoon, remove to paper towels to drain briefly. Serve immediately with the Yogurt Sauce for dipping.

Cabbie: Ahmed Hassan

Country of Origin: Egypt

Other Recipes:

Baklava (see page 174)

Yogurt Sauce

Ahmed seemed puzzled when asked if his yogurt sauce would be suitable for dipping raw vegetables. "We do not 'dip' vegetables," he answered. "I think this must be an American custom." A sauce like this one, he explains, usually accompanies a main dish as a condiment, much the same way as chutney or *raita*. "If there should be any 'dipping,' as you call it, we would use pieces of flat bread."

We suggest serving this with Jenail Singh's *Pakoras* (see page 33).

MAKES ABOUT 2 CUPS

1 cup plain low-fat yogurt

½ teaspoon freshly squeezed lemon juice

⅛ teaspoon salt

1 medium-size tomato, peeled, seeded, and finely chopped (see Note, page 122)

1 small yellow onion, minced (about ¼ cup)

1 small carrot, scraped, trimmed, and shredded (about ¼ cup)

¼ cup finely chopped cucumber

¼ cup finely chopped red or green bell pepper

1 tablespoon minced cilantro

In a small bowl, combine the yogurt, lemon juice, and salt. Stir in the tomato, onion, carrot, cucumber, bell pepper, and cilantro. Turn into a serving bowl and chill in the refrigerator for 1 or 2 hours until ready to serve.

TAXI TRIVIA: Seventy percent of taxicab passengers are Manhattan residents; seventeen percent are tourists.

Chapter 2 Appetizers and First Courses Meat and Poultry Fish and Seafood Hearty Soups and Stews Casseroles and Skillet Meals Side Dishes and Salads Breads and Baked Goods Desserts and Other Sweet Things Appetizers and First Courses Meat and Poultry Fish and Seafood Hearty Soups and Stews Casseroles and Skillet Meals Side Dishes and Salads Breads and Baked Goods Desserts and Other Sweet Things Appetizers and First Courses Meat and Poultry Fish and Seafood Hearty Soups and Stews Casseroles and Skillet Meals Side Dishes and Salads Breads and Baked Goods Desserts Other Sweet Things Appetizers and First Courses Meat and Poultry Fish and Seafood Hearty Soups and Stews Casseroles and Skillet Meals Side Dishes and Salads Breads and Baked Goods Desserts Other Sweet Things Appetizers and First Courses Meat and Poultry Fish and Seafood Hearty Soups and Stews Casseroles and Skillet Meals Side Dishes and Salads Breads and Baked Goods Desserts and Other Sweet Things Appetizers and First Courses Meat and Poultry Fish and Seafood Hearty Soups and Stews Casseroles and Skillet Meals Side Dishes and Salads Breads and Baked Goods Desserts and Other Sweet Things Appetizers and First Courses **Meat and Poultry** Fish and Seafood Hearty Soups and Stews Casseroles and Skillet Meals Side Dishes and Salads Breads and Baked Goods Desserts and Other Sweet Things Appetizers and First Courses Meat and Poultry Fish and Seafood Hearty Soups and Stews Casseroles and Skillet Meals Side Dishes and Salads Breads Baked Goods Desserts and Other Sweet Things Appetizers and First Courses Meat and Poultry Fish and Seafood Hearty Soups and Stews Casseroles and Skillet Meals Side Dishes and Salads Breads and Baked Goods Desserts and Other Sweet Things Appetizers and First Courses Meat and Poultry Fish and Seafood Hearty Soups and Stews Casseroles and Skillet Meals Side Dishes and Salads Breads and Baked Goods Desserts and Other Sweet Things Appetizers and First Courses Meat and Poultry Fish and Seafood Hearty Soups and Stews Casseroles and Skillet Meals Side Dishes Salads Breads and Baked Goods Desserts and Other Sweet Things Appetizers and First Courses Meat and Poultry Fish and Seafood Hearty Soups and Stews Casseroles and Skillet Meals Side Dishes and Salads Breads and Baked Goods Desserts and Other Sweet Things Appetizers and First Courses Meat and Poultry Fish and Seafood Hearty Soups and Stews Casseroles and Skillet Meals Side Dishes and Salads Breads and Baked Goods Desserts and Other Sweet Things Appetizers and First Courses Meat and Poultry Fish and Seafood Hearty Soups and Stews Casseroles and Skillet Meals Side Dishes and Salads Breads and Baked Goods Desserts and Other Sweet Things Appetizers and First Courses Meat and Poultry Fish and Seafood Hearty Soups and Stews Casseroles and Skillet Meals Side Dishes and Salads Breads and Baked Goods Desserts and Other Sweet Things Appetizers and First Courses Meat and Poultry Fish and Seafood Hearty Soups and Stews Casseroles and Skillet Meals Side Dishes and Salads Breads and Baked Goods Desserts and Other Sweet Things

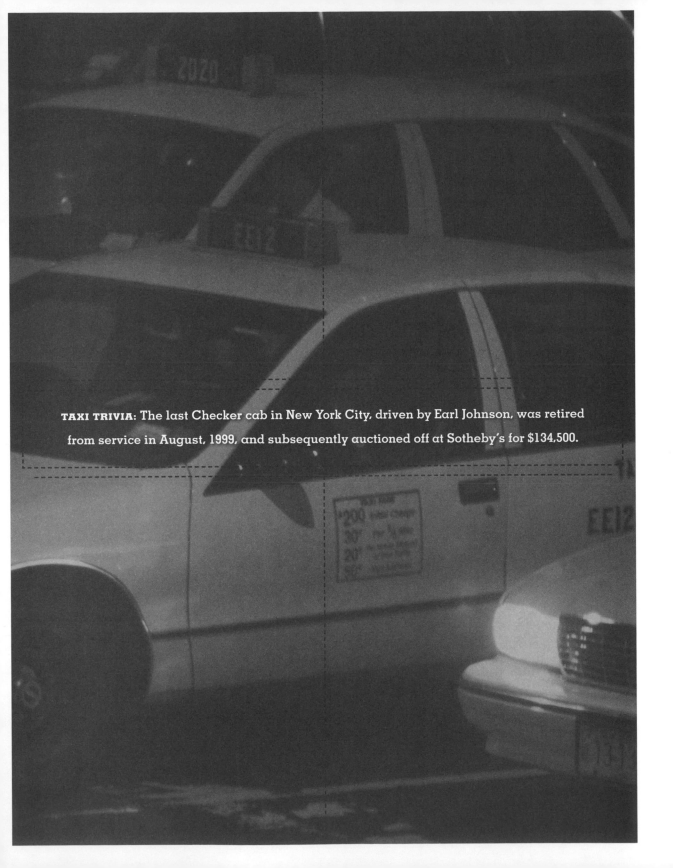

TAXI TRIVIA: The last Checker cab in New York City, driven by Earl Johnson, was retired from service in August, 1999, and subsequently auctioned off at Sotheby's for $134,500.

Cabbie: **Enoch Klinger**
Country of Origin: United States

Other Recipes:
Golden Corn Bread (see page 169)

PROFILE: Enoch was originally in the fur business, and he started to drive a cab on Saturday nights to pick up a little extra cash. He is retired now, and leases out his cab. "I get a nice check. I raise show cats now. I don't know why that always surprises people."

MEMORABLE FARES: Jackie Onassis, Senator Jacob Javitz, and John F. Kennedy, Jr. His most memorable fare was when he took his very pregnant wife to a movie. Just when the film was getting good, her water broke. He raced her to the hospital in his cab, but it turned out that they could have stuck around for the ending—she didn't give birth for another seventy-two hours.

Roast Beef
with Cold Tomato Salad

For those of the old school who believe that a rib roast should be cooked in an open pan with no liquid, Enoch urges them to try it his way—just once. The meat can still be served rare or medium-rare, if that's the way you like it, he points out, and the pan sauce, he says, makes wonderful gravy. The potatoes, lightly mashed with a fork, will be delicately flavored with the tomato sauce and meat juices. "To go with this dish," he adds, "besides my Tomato Salad, I would make pearl onions and peas."

MAKES 8 SERVINGS

3-pound boneless rib roast, rolled and tied

2 cloves garlic, slivered

4 baking potatoes (about 2 pounds), peeled and
  cut into quarters

1 (15-ounce) can tomato sauce

½ cup dry red wine

Freshly ground black pepper

Cold Tomato Salad, for serving
  (recipe follows)

1 Position a rack in the center of the oven. Preheat the oven to 550°F. With the tip of a skewer or a sharp knife, poke several ½-inch-deep holes evenly distributed in the fat-covered top side of the roast. Insert a garlic sliver into each hole.

2 Place the potatoes in a large saucepan, and cover with lightly salted water. Bring to a boil, then lower the heat, cover, and simmer briskly until the potatoes are half-tender, about 15 minutes. Drain and set aside.

3 Pour the tomato sauce in a roasting pan. Set the roast in the center of the pan in the sauce and arrange the drained potatoes around it. Pour the wine over the roast. Grind a generous amount of pepper over the meat and the potatoes.

4 Cover the pan tightly with foil and place it in the oven. Immediately lower the oven temperature to 350°F. It will take about 25 minutes per pound for rare; 30 to 35 minutes per pound for medium; and 40 to 45 minutes per pound for well done. However, to be sure, uncover and begin checking with an instant-read thermometer inserted into the center of the meat after it has roasted for about 40 minutes. (It should register 150°F for medium-rare, 160°F for medium, and 170°F for well done. Keep in mind that the meat will continue to cook some after it is removed from the oven, so consider it done when the thermometer registers about 5°F less than the desired temperature.) Leave the pan uncovered and continue to roast, turning and basting the potatoes several times with the tomato sauce, and checking the temperature of the meat at the same time.

5 Transfer the meat to a platter. Cover with foil and let stand for 15 minutes before carving. Skim off most of the fat from the sauce remaining in the roasting pan. Set the pan over two stovetop burners, and reheat the sauce and the potatoes just before serving.

6 To serve, carve the meat into slices and serve with the potatoes and pan sauce.

Cold Tomato Salad

"Don't forget to set the kitchen timer when you put the cans of tomatoes in the freezer," warns Enoch. "Otherwise you may end up with tomato slush." Along with the salad, you can offer a bowl of bite-size pieces of crisp lettuce on which to serve it.

MAKES 8 SERVINGS

4 (14½-ounce) cans diced tomatoes
1 onion (Walla Walla, Spanish, Vidalia,
 or other mild onion), cut in half through
 the stem, then cut into very thin
 vertical slices
Freshly ground black pepper, to taste
Extra-virgin olive oil
Red wine vinegar
Kosher or coarse salt

1 Open the cans of tomatoes and drain off most of the liquid. Set the tomatoes (in the cans) in the freezer for 30 to 40 minutes, or until they are very cold but not starting to freeze.

2 Turn the chilled tomatoes and the remaining liquid into a salad bowl. Toss with the onion, then season generously with pepper. Serve the salad with cruets of olive oil and vinegar, as well as coarse salt to be added to taste at the table. Refrigerate if not serving immediately, but not for too long, as the onion will become limp.

Cabbie: **Victor Babicz**

Country of Origin: Argentina

Other Recipes:

Madambre: Steak Roll Stuffed with Diced Vegetable Salad (see page 22)

"Chimichurri"

Steak with Parsley and Garlic Sauce

Argentineans love their beef—grilled, roasted, barbecued, or fried—which they traditionally serve with a variety of sauces that are eaten with the meat. This spicy combination of parsley, garlic, and vinegar is particularly popular. Victor says he likes to accompany his beef with a salad made with more or less equal parts of sliced radishes, chopped juicy tomatoes, chopped watercress, and chopped scallions, seasoned to taste with salt and freshly ground pepper but no dressing. He also sets out thick slices of crusty bread, which are dipped into the mixture of beef juices and sauce that collect on the dinner plate.

MAKES ABOUT ⅔ CUP;

4 GENEROUS SERVINGS OF SAUCE

1 cup minced fresh parsley

6 to 8 cloves garlic, minced

2 teaspoons dried oregano leaves, crumbled

2 teaspoons crushed red pepper flakes

½ cup red wine vinegar

½ cup water

6 tablespoons canola
  or other vegetable oil

Salt and freshly ground black pepper

Choice or Prime steak (sirloin, porterhouse, t-bone,
  or strip) for four servings, broiled

1 In a small bowl, combine the parsley, garlic, oregano, red pepper, vinegar, and water. Gradually whisk in the oil and beat for about 30 seconds until slightly thickened. Season with salt and pepper. Although this sauce is best just after it's made, it can be stored in the refrigerator in a tightly covered container for up to 3 days. Bring to room temperature and beat briefly before serving.

2 Serve the sauce alongside the prepared steak.

Cabbies: **Anna and Peter Egan**

Country of Origin: Ireland and the United States

Other Recipes:

Irish Lamb Stew (see page 106)

Mashed Potatoes, Carrots, and Parsnips (see page 147)

Irish Soda Bread (see page 170)

Emerald Isle Trifle (see page 189)

PROFILE: This taxi-driving couple worked different shifts for nearly twenty years while they were raising their five children. "We almost never saw each other, although we always took the weekend off to be together. It was worth it. The kids have always come first with us and they've turned out well."

BEING A CABBIE: Peter has been driving a cab for more than forty years. Though semi-retired now, Peter still takes the cab out now and then because he enjoys driving and meeting new people. "Early on, I discovered that people who've had a wee bit too much to drink, and a fellow trying to impress his girl, are the best tippers. My philosophy has always been that if you're really interested in who's riding in the back seat, they take to you and show you their best side."

MOST MEMORABLE FARES: Dick Cavett (three times), Elizabeth Taylor, and Jackie Leonard, who delivered one-liners non-stop throughout the ride; and a not-famous passenger clutching a finger he'd just cut off—he calmly asked to be taken to a nearby hospital.

ABOUT NEW YORK/AMERICA: "On the whole, driving a cab in New York has been a nice experience. Passengers offer you food, coffee, and magazines and are generally very courteous and considerate."

Glazed Corned Beef with Vegetables

"Both Peter and I enjoy cooking and shopping for food," says Anna, "and we like putting a little twist on the old-country recipes, like glazing this corned beef with a brown sugar mixture that includes a splash of Irish whiskey."

MAKES 6 SERVINGS

1 corned beef brisket (about 4 pounds)	**Glaze**
2 bay leaves	½ cup packed dark brown sugar
8 whole peppercorns	1½ teaspoons dry mustard
2 whole allspice	2 tablespoons unsulfured molasses
2-inch cinnamon stick	2 tablespoons Irish whiskey
1 teaspoon yellow mustard seeds	or orange juice

Vegetables

12 tiny new potatoes, scrubbed

18 peeled baby carrots

1 large Savoy or green cabbage, cut into 8 wedges

12 large scallions, including most of the green tops, trimmed

1 Place the corned beef, fat-side up, in a Dutch oven or other large, heavy stew pot. Add enough cold water to cover the meat by about 2 inches. Heat to boiling over high heat, skimming off the foam as it rises to the surface. Lower the heat until the water barely simmers. Add the bay leaves, peppercorns, allspice, cinnamon stick, and mustard seeds. Cover, and cook until fork-tender, about 3 hours. (The meat will have shrunk quite a lot.)

2 While the corned beef is cooking, prepare the Glaze. In a small bowl, combine the brown sugar, dry mustard, molasses, and whiskey, and set aside.

3 Preheat the oven to 375°F. Lift the corned beef from the Dutch oven, reserving the cooking liquid, and transfer it to a small baking pan, fat-side up. Pour 1 cup of the reserved cooking liquid into the roasting pan, and reserve the remaining liquid in the Dutch oven. Spoon about half of the glaze on top of the corned beef, spreading it evenly. Bake for 20 to 25 minutes, spreading the remaining glaze over the meat about halfway through baking time. Remove from the oven, cover, and keep warm until the vegetables have finished cooking, if necessary.

4 While the corned beef is baking, prepare the Vegetables: Bring the liquid remaining in the Dutch oven to a slow boil. Add the potatoes and carrots, and cook, uncovered, for 15 minutes. Add the cabbage and scallions, and cook for 10 minutes longer, or until all the vegetables are tender.

5 To serve, slice the meat across the grain and arrange it on a serving platter. Drain the vegetables and arrange them around the meat. Pour the juices that have accumulated in the roasting pan over the meat and vegetables.

TAXI TRIVIA: Of the approximately forty thousand licensed cab drivers in NYC, only about 1.1 percent are women.

Cabbie: **Mikiel Elchine**

Country of Origin: Russia

Beef Stroganoff

"I almost never find a *stroganov* in this country that in any way resembles the one my mother used to make in Russia," Mikiel laments. "This recipe, which I worked out myself, tastes the same way my mother's did. Rice is the correct accompaniment for *stroganov*," he adds, "but I know most Americans prefer noodles. I like to serve this dish with a very simple green salad as a first course, and a Georgian red wine or Cabernet."

MAKES 4 TO 6 SERVINGS

2 cups beef broth (see page 92)

1 pound beef tenderloin

3 tablespoons vegetable oil

3 tablespoons butter

¾ pound small white mushrooms, trimmed, rinsed, patted dry, and thinly sliced

8 small yellow onions (about 1¼ pounds), thinly sliced

½ teaspoon freshly ground black pepper

1½ cups regular sour cream

Salt, to taste

Hot cooked white rice or egg noodles

Chopped fresh parsley, for garnish

1 In a small saucepan, boil the beef broth until it is reduced to 1 cup. Remove from the heat and set aside.

2 Cut the beef into strips about the size of thin French fries. The easiest way to do this is to cut the tenderloin crosswise into ¼-inch slices, then, going with the grain of the meat, cut the slices into ¼-inch strips.

3 Heat 1 tablespoon of the oil and 1 tablespoon of the butter in a large skillet or a high-sided sauté pan set over high heat. When the oil and butter sizzles, stir in the mushrooms and onions. Cook, stirring almost constantly, until the mushrooms have started to give up their liquid and the mixture is steaming. Reduce the heat to low. Cover and cook, stirring occasionally, until both the mushrooms and the onions are very tender, about 10 minutes. Uncover and continue to cook, stirring, until most of the liquid in the pan has evaporated. Turn the mushroom mixture into a large bowl and set aside.

4 Wipe the skillet with paper towels and set it over high heat. Add 1 tablespoon of the remaining butter and 1 tablespoon of the remaining oil. When the butter and oil are sizzling, add about half the beef strips, and cook over high heat, tossing and turning them until they are lightly browned on all sides. Remove the meat to the bowl containing the mushroom mixture. Add the remaining butter and oil to the skillet, and repeat the browning process with the remaining meat. Transfer the meat to the bowl.

5 Discard the grease in the skillet and return it to high heat. Stir the broth into the hot skillet, scraping up any crusty, brown bits that stick to the bottom. Boil the broth for about 3 minutes until it has reduced slightly. Add the reserved beef-and-mushroom mixture, and cook over medium-low heat, stirring constantly, until the mixture is hot. Reduce the heat to low, and stir in the sour cream by the spoonful until the mixture is well blended. Cook gently for 2 to 3 minutes, stirring constantly, until the sauce is heated through. (If the sauce is allowed to boil, the sour cream will curdle, so watch carefully.) Season with salt.

6 Serve the stroganoff over rice or noodles, sprinkled with parsley.

BIG APPLE BITE: It's long been believed that New York was nicknamed "The Big Apple" by jazz musicians who regarded a gig in Harlem to be a sign that they had made it. It turns out that it had actually first appeared in the 1920s when reporter John Fitzgerald, who reported on horse races for the *Morning Telegraph*, referred to the New York racetrack. Apparently, stable hands in New Orleans called a trip to a New York racetrack the "Big Apple"—or the sweet reward—for any talented thoroughbred. The term passed into popular usage long after the racetrack disappeared.

Cabbie: **David Newman**
Country of Origin: United States

Esther Newman's Meat Loaf

"My mom used to make the best meat loaf," David recalls. "She served it with mashed potatoes, gravy, and a salad with a dressing made by mixing catsup, mayonnaise, and a little vinegar. Mom doesn't cook anymore, but I know how to make her meat loaf."

This may be one of the best meat loaves we've ever tasted. It is moist and very flavorful, and is just as good—maybe better—served cold. For a change, you can substitute about four whole hard-cooked eggs for the dill pickles in the center of the loaf.

Makes 6 to 8 servings

1 cup whole milk

3 slices slightly dry firm bread, pulled into small pieces

1½ pounds ground beef

½ cup finely chopped dill pickle

1 medium-size yellow onion, finely chopped (about ½ cup)

¼ cup chopped fresh parsley

2 teaspoons Worcestershire sauce

1 large egg, lightly beaten

½ teaspoon salt

½ teaspoon garlic powder

¼ teaspoon freshly ground black pepper

3 whole dill pickles, each as straight as possible and about 4 inches long

Chili sauce (optional)

1 Preheat the oven to 350°F (325°F if using a glass loaf pan). Lightly grease a loaf pan and set aside.

2 In a large bowl, combine the milk and the bread, and let stand for 5 minutes. Add the ground beef, chopped pickle, onion, parsley, Worcestershire sauce, egg, salt, garlic powder, and pepper. With your hands, mix gently until thoroughly blended. (Try not to handle the mixture any more than necessary.)

3 Gently press half of the meat mixture into the bottom of the prepared loaf pan. Arrange the pickles down the center of the loaf, trimming the ends, if necessary, to make them fit. Cover with the remaining meat mixture, patting it down gently but firmly, making sure that it completely encloses the pickles.

4 Bake the meat loaf for 60 minutes, or until the juices bubbling up in the pan are clear. Midway through baking time, spread the top of the loaf with the chili sauce, if desired. After removing from the oven, let the meat loaf rest for about 10 minutes, then drain off the fat and juices, which can be used to make gravy. To serve, cut the meat loaf into slices.

TAXI TRIVIA: The word "cab" comes from the French word "*cabriolet*," meaning horse-drawn cart; the word "taxi" comes from another French word, "*taximeter*," meaning fare meter. Cabs become known as "taxicabs" or "taxis" after newly invented meters were installed in the early 1900s.

Cabbie: **David Ghalian**

Country of Origin: Jordan

Other Recipes:

Meloukhiah: Chicken with Chopped Collard Greens and Garlic (see page 69)

Sarata: White Bean Salad (see page 158)

ABOUT NEW YORK/AMERICA: "I love everything about America, but I do miss some of the food from Jordan."

"Kofta"

Egg-shaped Meatballs with Tomato Rice

"This dish is very popular where I come from. I like it so much that my wife makes it for me almost every two days. And please try my *Sarata* (see page 158), which is very good with this."

MAKES 6 SERVINGS

1 pound ground lamb (not too lean; 20 to 25 percent fat)

4 slices slightly dry, firm bread, crusts removed and pulled into tiny pieces

1 medium-size yellow onion, minced (about ½ cup)

2 tablespoons finely chopped fresh parsley

1 tablespoon finely chopped fresh mint

¾ teaspoon salt

¼ teaspoon freshly ground black pepper

2 tablespoons olive oil

1 cup raw converted white rice

2 or 3 medium-size tomatoes, peeled, seeded, cored, and chopped (about 1 cup; see Note, page 122)

1 In a large bowl, with your hands, gently mix together the ground lamb, bread, onion, parsley, mint, salt, and pepper until well combined. Using about ½ cup of the meat mixture for each patty, shape the mixture into 6 oval meatballs.

2 Heat the oil in a large skillet set over high heat. When the oil is very hot, fry the patties over medium-high heat until they are nicely browned and slightly crusty on all sides, 3 to 4 minutes. Reduce the heat to medium-low, partially cover, and continue to cook, turning occasionally, until just cooked through, about 10 minutes.

3 Meanwhile, cook the rice as the package directs for firmer rice. When the rice is removed from the heat, stir in the tomatoes and fluff the rice. Cover and let stand for 5 minutes. Serve the meatballs accompanied by the rice.

Cabbie: **Steve Kosefas**

Country of Origin: Greece

Other Recipes:

Avgolemono: Greek Egg and Lemon Soup with Chicken (see page 95)

Tomatoes Stuffed with Chopped Lamb and Rice (see page 120)

"Arnaki Fornou"

Greek-style Roast Leg of Lamb

Lamb is the meat most closely associated with Greek cooking, especially at Easter, when the aroma of spit-roasting lamb covers the land, signaling the end of the Lenten fast. The Easter lamb is almost always served with "Easter salad," a mixture of romaine lettuce and scallion shreds, chopped fresh dill sprigs, and a dressing made with a mixture of olive oil, lemon juice, and salt and pepper to taste. "We eat as much lettuce as we can in the spring," says Steve, "because during the hot summer, when tomatoes, cucumbers, and bell peppers are abundant, the lettuce is long gone, which is why a 'real' Greek salad never has any lettuce in it.

"Like most Greeks, I like my lamb a little on the well-done side, but I know most Americans prefer to eat it medium or even medium-rare."

Preparation for this recipe must be started 24 hours before serving.

MAKES 10 TO 12 SERVINGS

Whole leg of lamb (6 to 9 pounds), shank bone
   cracked for easier handling
3 cloves garlic, cut into thin slivers
½ cup olive oil
½ cup freshly squeezed lemon juice
3 teaspoons dried oregano leaves, crumbled
Kosher salt and freshly ground black pepper
½ cup boiling water
Lemon halves, for garnish

1 The day before roasting, with the tip of a paring knife, make many small slits down into the meat through the fat side of the lamb. Insert a sliver of garlic into each slit. (This will take some time, but the more slits, the more the flavor of the garlic and other seasonings will permeate the meat.)

2 In a small bowl, combine the olive oil, lemon juice, and oregano. Brush about half of this mixture evenly over the top of the lamb, then season with the salt and pepper, rubbing it in well. Place the lamb in a roasting pan. Cover, and refrigerate overnight or up to 24 hours. Also cover and refrigerate the remaining oil mixture.

3 Preheat the oven to 325°F. Uncover the lamb, and roast it for 1 hour. Drain or siphon off any fat that has accumulated in the pan. Add the hot water to the reserved oil-and-lemon-juice mixture, and pour into the roasting pan. Continue to roast the lamb, basting every 20 to 30 minutes with the juices that accumulate in the roasting pan. Figure on about 20 to 25 minutes per pound, or until a meat thermometer inserted in the thickest part of the lamb, not touching fat or bone, registers 150°F for medium-rare, 160°F for medium, or 170°F for well done. Set the lamb aside for about 20 minutes before carving.

4 To serve the roast in the true Greek fashion, surround it with lemon halves to be squeezed over the carved lamb to each diner's taste.

Cabbie: **Mughal Iqbal**

Country of Origin: Lebanon

Baked Breast of Lamb
with Butter Beans and Mint Tea

One of the important things Mughal brought with him, he says, is this recipe for a special way of cooking lamb. "Meat closest to the bone is the tastiest," he says, "and you will believe that after you eat my lamb. I would suggest drinking mint tea with this meal. In fact, I will give you my recipe for that, too" (recipe follows).

MAKES 4 SERVINGS

---

2 half-breasts of lamb (about 1½ pounds each), each cut in half between the ribs to make a total of 4 pieces

Salt and freshly ground black pepper, to taste

1 (14½-ounce) can diced tomatoes, drained, the juice reserved

3 tablespoons tomato paste

½ teaspoon dry mustard

⅛ teaspoon cayenne pepper

1 tablespoon olive oil or vegetable oil

1 medium-size yellow onion, chopped (about ½ cup)

3 cloves garlic, minced

2 (15-ounce) cans butter beans (lima beans), rinsed and drained

Chopped fresh parsley, for garnish

1 Preheat the oven to 450°F. Trim most of the fat from the tops of the pieces of lamb breast, and generously season both sides with salt and pepper. Arrange the breast pieces, meaty-side down, in a roasting pan that is just large enough to hold them in one layer. Place the lamb in the oven and roast for 20 minutes; turn the lamb meaty-side up and roast for 10 minutes longer. Remove from the oven and set aside. Reduce the oven heat to 350°F.

2 Add enough water to the reserved tomato liquid to make 1 cup. In a small bowl,

stir together the tomato liquid, tomato paste, dry mustard, and cayenne until well blended; set aside.

3 Heat the oil in a large skillet over high heat. When it is hot, stir in the onion and garlic. Cook over medium-high heat, stirring almost constantly, until the onion and garlic have softened and started to brown, about 5 minutes. Stir in the tomato-juice mixture and continue to cook until the mixture is simmering. Remove from the heat and stir in the chopped tomato.

4 Remove the lamb from the roasting pan and set aside. Discard all of the fat in the pan, but leave any dark juices and crusty brown bits that cling to the bottom of the pan. Stir the tomato mixture into the roasting pan. Add the beans, and stir gently until they are well coated with pan drippings. Return the lamb to the roasting pan, arranging the pieces over the beans, meaty-side up. Continue to bake for 30 minutes.

5 To serve, place the pieces of lamb over the beans on a large platter, and sprinkle with the parsley.

Mint Tea

MAKES ABOUT 6 CUPS

5 cups water
1½ cups bruised mint leaves
  (to bruise the leaves, roll them between the palms
  of your hands)
½ cup sugar
1 tablespoon pekoe (Ceylon) tea leaves

In a medium-size, non-metallic saucepan, stir together the water, mint leaves, sugar, and tea leaves. Set the pan over high heat and bring to a boil. Immediately remove from the heat, and cover tightly. Set aside to steep for about 5 minutes. Meanwhile, rinse a teapot with hot water to warm it. Strain the tea into the warmed teapot. Serve in juice glasses or teacups.

BIG APPLE BITE: New Yorkers refer to Manhattan as "the City," even though it's an island, and "the Island" translates to Long Island.

Cabbie: **Mohammed Akbar**

Country of Origin: Afghanistan

Other Recipes:

Perfectly Cooked Basmati Rice (see page 149)

Lamb Shanks with Rice Palau and Yogurt Chutney

"Drink green tea with this meal," advises Mohammed. "Tea is good with fatty foods. It makes the grease go down better. If you drink water or soda, it will make you feel full when you are not." In addition to the rice and chutney, Mohammed also highly recommends setting a bowl of *achchar* on the table. "These are spicy mixed pickles you can buy at Middle Eastern grocery stores," he says.

MAKES 4 SERVINGS

4 meaty lamb shanks (¾ to 1 pound each)
Salt and freshly ground black pepper
¼ cup vegetable oil
I large yellow onion, finely chopped (about 1 cup)
½ cup coarsely chopped cilantro leaves
1 to 2 teaspoons mild curry powder
½ cup water

Rice Palau
1 recipe Perfectly Cooked Basmati Rice
  (followed through step 2, page 149)
¼ cup water
2 tablespoons sugar

Yogurt Chutney
2 tablespoons chopped cilantro sprigs and
  tender stems
1 clove garlic, minced
1½ teaspoons white vinegar
1 cup plain yogurt
Salt, to taste
½ teaspoon minced hot green chile pepper
  (optional)

1 Trim away any excess fat on the lamb shanks, then season them generously with salt and pepper. Place the oil in a Dutch oven or other large, heavy stew pot set over high heat. When the oil is hot, add the lamb shanks and cook, turning the shanks and adjusting the heat as necessary, until they are lightly browned on all sides. With tongs, remove the shanks and set aside.

2 In the oil remaining in the pan, cook the onion over medium-high heat, stirring almost constantly, just until slightly softened. Stir in the cilantro, curry powder, and water. Return the lamb shanks to the pot, spooning the onion mixture over them. Cover tightly, and cook over low heat until the shanks are very tender, 1 to 1¼ hours.

3 Meanwhile, prepare the Rice Palau: Follow the instructions given for Perfectly

Cooked Basmati Rice through Step 2. In Step 3, preheat the oven to 500°F as directed. Return the rice to the same heavy saucepan in which it was cooked, and gently shape it into a mound, leaving a little space around the rice in the bottom of the pan.

4 Place the water and sugar in a small, heavy saucepan and bring to a boil over high heat. Simmer briskly until the mixture is reduced to a brown syrup, about 5 minutes. Starting at the top of the mound, immediately drizzle the syrup over and around the rice. (The syrup will seep through the mound, resulting in a multicolored rice after it is steamed.) Pour the remaining ¼ cup of water *around* the rice, not over it. Cover the pan tightly and place it in the oven for 10 minutes. Turn off the oven and leave the pan in the oven for an additional 10 minutes.

5 Meanwhile, prepare the Yogurt Chutney: Chop the cilantro and garlic together until very finely minced, almost to a purée. Scrape the cilantro mixture into a small bowl. Stir in the white vinegar (just enough to moisten the mixture), and then the yogurt, salt, and chile pepper, if using. Cover, and chill until ready to serve.

6 To serve, mound the Rice Palau on a large platter and arrange the lamb shanks around it. Spoon some of the pan juices over the lamb and serve the rest on the side. Accompany with the Yogurt Chutney.

BIG APPLE BITE: According to the 2000 Census,
there are 66,834 people per square mile in the Big Apple.

Cabbie: **Jeffrey Fares**
Country of Origin: Egypt

Lamb Shish Kabob

"In Egypt, men don't cook, but here things are different, especially since I am married to an American," says Jeffrey. "This is one of my favorite dishes. My mother gave me the recipe, which is very famous all over the world, a skewered combination of colorful vegetables and tasty chunks of tender lamb that have been marinated for a couple of days. For the best flavor, kabobs should be cooked over charcoal. Egyptians like meat well done, but I know that Americans like some pink in the middle. Sometimes my wife cooks this, and sometimes I do, depending on who has time. My kids really love it." To drink with the kabobs, Jeffrey suggests a good Egyptian red wine, such as Omir Kayam.

Preparation for this recipe must begin at least 24 hours in advance, and preferably 48 hours, to marinate.

MAKES 4 SKEWERS; 4 SERVINGS

1 small yellow onion, minced (about ¼ cup)

3 tablespoons red wine vinegar

2 tablespoons extra-virgin olive oil

½ teaspoon ground cumin

½ teaspoon salt

¼ teaspoon pepper

2 pounds boneless leg of lamb cut into cubes (you will need twenty 1½-inch lamb cubes)

1 large red onion

2 large, firm, ripe tomatoes, or 8 cherry tomatoes

1 large red bell pepper, cored, seeded, halved, and each half cut into 4 squares

1 large green bell pepper, cored, seeded, halved, and each half cut into 4 squares

8 large white or crimini mushrooms, stems trimmed and discarded, rinsed, and patted dry with paper towels

Hot cooked couscous, or white or brown rice, for serving

1 In a large bowl, whisk together the minced onion, vinegar, olive oil, cumin, salt, and pepper. Add the lamb cubes, and turn until each piece is well coated with the marinade. Cover, and refrigerate for 24 to 48 hours, stirring the mixture every now and then.

2 Cut the onions in half through the stem, and trim the ends. Separate the onion into layers; cut the layers into 1¼-inch squares.

3 Cut the tomatoes into quarters (if using cherry tomatoes, leave them whole). Have ready four 8-inch metal skewers.

4 Remove the lamb from the marinade. Wipe off any bits of onion clinging to the cubes and discard the marinade. To assemble the kabobs: There will be 5 pieces of lamb on each skewer, beginning and ending with the lamb. Between the cubes of lamb, skewer 2 pieces of red pepper, 2 pieces of green pepper, 2 mushrooms, 2 pieces of onion, and 2 tomato quarters (or a whole cherry tomato) in an attractive, alternating pattern. Cover, and refrigerate until ready to grill. (The kabobs can be prepared several hours in advance, up to this point.)

5 Prepare a medium-hot charcoal grill. Grill the kabobs 4 to 6 inches above the coals for about 10 minutes, turning frequently, until the lamb is pink in the center and the vegetables are tender. (Alternatively, the kabobs can be oven-broiled about 4 inches below the source of heat for about 6 minutes, turning once.)

6 To serve, push the meat and vegetables off the skewer and onto dinner plates. Serve with couscous, or white or brown rice.

BIG APPLE BITE: New York City has more than 20,000 restaurants, representing nearly every one of the world's cuisines. The largest is the Bryant Park Grill, which seats 1,420 people.

Cabbie: **Dedi Sharif**
Country of Origin: Indonesia

Other Recipes:

Perkedel Jagong: Fried Corn Cakes (see page 145)
Cucumber Salad (see page 157)

Lamb Satay

"My wife, who is German and works for the United Nations, loves the way I make satay," says Dedi, "but like most people who are not used to eating food from a stick, she has trouble with them. The easiest way, I tell her, is to nibble the meat right off the skewer, which is the way we Indonesians do it."

The satay that Dedi prepares at home is nearly identical to the kabobs that cart vendors sell on street corners. (Your nose—and a line of off-duty taxicabs—will lead you to the man selling satays, since the aroma of these spicy-sweet Indonesian kabobs cooking over charcoal is nothing short of divine, and they are a lunch favorite for many cabbies.) Most often satay is made with lamb, as these are, but beef or chicken can be easily substituted.

We liked these kabobs served with packaged butter-and-garlic-flavored rice. If you prefer to make your own version of this flavorful rice from scratch, cook plain, long-grain rice according to package directions. Just before serving, stir in a skillet sauce made by cooking minced garlic in bubbling-hot butter just until golden.

Kecap manis, a sweet, thick soy sauce, is an important ingredient called for in this recipe.

MAKES 4 SERVINGS

---

1 pound lean, boneless lamb, cut into ½-inch cubes
1 medium-size yellow onion, shredded (about ½ cup)
1 teaspoon minced garlic
2 tablespoons **kecap manis** (available in Asian markets and gourmet stores)
½ teaspoon ground coriander
¼ teaspoon ground turmeric
1 tablespoon packed dark brown sugar
1 tablespoon peanut oil
Cucumber Salad (see page 157), for serving
1 (6.2-ounce) package garlic-and-butter rice (such as Uncle Ben's), cooked as directed, for serving

1 Place the lamb in a medium-size bowl. In a small bowl, combine the onion, garlic, *kecap manis*, coriander, turmeric, brown sugar, and oil until the mixture forms a paste. Stir this mixture into the lamb cubes until they are well coated. Cover, and refrigerate for several hours, then bring to room temperature for about 1 hour before cooking. Place 8 wooden skewers in a bowl of cold water and set aside while the lamb is marinating. (Soaking them prevents the skewers from burning on the grill.)

2 Prepare a medium-hot charcoal grill. Remove the skewers from the water and pat dry on paper towels. On a large sheet of waxed paper, divide the lamb cubes into 4 equal portions. Thread one portion of lamb cubes on each skewer, placing them very close to one another. Arrange the skewers on the grill, and cook for about 2 minutes on each side for medium-rare, or until the meat is done as you like it. (Alternatively, the kabobs can be oven-broiled about 4 inches below the source of heat for about the same amount of time.) Serve immediately with the Cucumber Salad and garlic-and-butter rice.

Cabbie: **Iqbal Khan**

Country of Origin: Pakistan

Pakistani Curried Lamb

Iqbal prefers goat meat for his curry, but admits that it is hard to find in this country. "But neck of lamb will do just fine," says this cabbie, who is presently studying advanced digital electronics. "In honesty, most Americans are not accustomed to goat meat and usually do not like it. I think this is a meat that you must eat since childhood in order to enjoy it. The exception may be my wife. Although she is Italian, she begs me to make this recipe using goat meat if I can find it. Before the start of every meal we both say '*Bismillah*,' which means 'Start with the name of Almighty God.'"

We liked the hint of sweetness a little mango chutney provides to this dish. A bowl of *Raita* (see page 161) would be a nice complement, as well. We chose lightly steamed and buttered spinach to complete the meal.

MAKES 4 TO 6 SERVINGS

2 tablespoons vegetable oil

2 medium-size yellow onions, cut in half through the stem and the halves cut into thin vertical slices

2 cloves garlic, minced

2-inch piece fresh ginger, peeled and shredded (discard the stringy pieces that collect on the outside of the grater)

6 cloves

6 small bay leaves

1 tablespoon cumin seed

2 to 2½ pounds lamb neck, cut into 2- to 3-inch chunks

1 teaspoon garam masala (available in Middle Eastern markets)

½ teaspoon ground coriander

1 cup cold water

Hot cooked basmati rice (see page 149)

¼ cup chopped cilantro, for garnish

Store-bought mango chutney, for serving

1 Heat the oil in a Dutch oven or other large, heavy stew pot over medium heat. When it is hot, add the onions and cook, stirring, until softened, 3 to 5 minutes. Stir in the garlic, ginger, cloves, bay leaves, and cumin seed, and cook briefly until the spices become very aromatic. Add the lamb, and cook, stirring and moving the meat around in the pan, until it has lost most of its raw color. Stir in the garam masala and coriander until well blended.

2 Add the water and bring the mixture to a boil. Reduce the heat, cover, and simmer slowly for about 45 minutes until the lamb is tender but not falling from the bones. Now and then, lift the lid and move the pieces of lamb around in the pot. (Toward the end of this cooking period, the bay leaves will have done their job and you can pick them out as they come to the surface.) Remove the lid and continue to cook for 15 to 20 minutes, stirring occasionally, until about half the liquid has evaporated and the pan juices are fairly thick. With a large spoon, skim the fat from the surface.

3 To serve, spoon the rice onto a large platter. Spoon the meat and sauce in the center of the rice. Sprinkle the cilantro over both the rice and the curry, and serve with mango chutney.

TAXI TRIVIA: Cars for hire with internal-combustion engines first gathered around The Plaza hotel at 59th Street and Fifth Avenue about 1905. The very first cabs, of course, were horse-drawn, known as "hansom cabs." In the early part of the 1900s, a fleet of electric-and-battery-powered autos were introduced, but these heavy vehicles, which were difficult to maneuver, didn't last long, and the end came in 1907 when their garage burned down.

Cabbie: **Awilda Velez**

Country of Origin: Puerto Rico

Other Recipes:

Sweet-spiced Papaya (see page 177)

PROFILE: "I came to this country when I was just nineteen years old. In Puerto Rico I had a good job as a supervisor of a sunglasses factory, but I wanted to spend more time with my young son, so my husband and I decided to come to New York and drive cabs. That way we could work different shifts and one of us would always be at home."

ABOUT NEW YORK/AMERICA: "Although the rest of our family is still in Puerto Rico, and even though I always said that cab driving would not be a lifetime job, we still love it here—except for the traffic of course—and we almost never speak of going back."

Adobo Pork Roast

Awilda serves her roast with yellow rice and pink beans, Boiled and Buttered Plantains (see page 156), and a green salad. "Vinegar," she says, "goes well with pork." So she adds two mellow vinegars to the pan drippings before making an American-style gravy. "You can add less vinegar, or none at all, if you don't like tartness in your gravy. We prefer to drink fresh fruit juice with our meals instead of wine."

Adobo seasoning, a common Hispanic ingredient called for in this recipe, is a salty, dry seasoning blend available in the spice section of virtually every supermarket. The brand with which we are most familiar is Goya. There are several blends, but the one used in this recipe and throughout the book is the plain seasoning blend with pepper.

Preparation for this recipe must be started at least 8 hours or the day before serving.

MAKES 6 TO 8 SERVINGS

1 medium-size yellow onion, shredded (about ½ cup)

½ cup minced cilantro

4 cloves garlic, minced

1 tablespoon adobo seasoning

1 rolled and tied boneless pork shoulder roast, weighing about 4 pounds

2 tablespoons cider vinegar, or to taste

2 tablespoons balsamic vinegar, or to taste

6 tablespoons all-purpose flour

1½ cups water

1️⃣ In a small bowl, mix together the onion, cilantro, garlic, and adobo seasoning to make a wet paste.

2️⃣ With a metal skewer, pierce the roast deeply on all sides many times. (If the roast is covered with elastic netting, remove it and retie the roast with string.) Rub the onion paste on all sides of the roast. Place the roast in a large, zipper-top plastic bag. Refrigerate for at least 8 hours or overnight, turning the bag frequently.

3 Preheat the oven to 350°F. Wipe off the excess onion paste from the roast. Place the roast on a rack in a shallow roasting pan. Cover the pan tightly (with aluminum foil, if necessary) and roast for 1 hour. Uncover and continue roasting for 45 minutes to 1 hour, or until an instant-read meat thermometer inserted in several places in the center of the roast registers 155°F. Remove the roast to a cutting board or platter, and cover with foil to keep warm while making the gravy.

4 To make the gravy, first remove the rack from the roasting pan. Pour off all but about ¼ cup of the fat, but leave the meat drippings and any crusty brown bits in the pan. Set the roasting pan over two burners over medium-high heat. Stir in both vinegars until well blended with the pan drippings. Meanwhile, in a small bowl, whisk the flour with the water until well blended. When the drippings simmer, whisk in the flour and water. Continue whisking until the mixture is simmering and quite thick. Keeping the gravy at a low boil, continue to whisk in water until the gravy is thick, smooth, and bubbly.

5 Cut the roast into slices and serve with gravy.

BIG APPLE BITE: Wall Street was not always home to the New York Stock Exchange. As a matter of fact, there was a wall there, erected in 1653 to protect the city from an unexpected attack.

Cabbie: George T. Ryan
Country of Origin: United States

PROFILE: It's not hard to believe that this debonair cab driver is a retired attorney and former judge. "After losing an election, I became discouraged with politics and decided to settle in New York, a place I'd always wanted to live. When I got here, I opted to drive a cab while I decided what to do with the rest of my life. As it turns out, I've found driving so enjoyable and have met so many interesting people that the only thing I've decided to do is let each day take care of itself and not worry about the future."

MEMORABLE FARES: A few years ago he picked up a couple, Don and Sally. Don was in town to edit a major motion picture, and Sally wanted to sightsee and shop while Don worked. George obliged, driving and accompanying Sally to fancy food markets, cookware stores, and wine shops all around Manhattan. The two, who shared a common love of cooking, soon become buddies and over the years the friendship has continued to blossom.

Pork Chops L'Orange

"This recipe evolved bit by bit from duck with orange sauce," says George, "one of my favorites when I was a budding cook. If orange was good with duck, I figured it would be good with chicken, and if it was good with chicken, it would probably work with pork, which it did, and this has since become one of my favorite company dishes."

Preparation for this recipe must be started at least 8 hours or the day before serving.

MAKES 6 SERVINGS

6 bone-in loin pork chops (8 to 10 ounces each)
3 cloves garlic, minced
1½ teaspoons salt
¾ teaspoon freshly ground black pepper
3 cups freshly squeezed orange juice
3 tablespoons butter
3 tablespoons vegetable oil
1 Vidalia or other sweet onion, finely chopped (about 1¼ cups)
12 ounces medium-size white mushrooms, stems discarded, and caps cut into thin slices
½ cup dry sherry or vermouth
1 (12-ounce) jar pork gravy
1 teaspoon grated orange zest
1 bay leaf

All-purpose flour, for dredging the chops
Chopped fresh parsley, for garnish
Ryan's Special Wild Rice (recipe follows), for serving

1 Trim the chops of any excess fat. In a small bowl, mix together the garlic, salt, pepper, and 2 teaspoons of the orange juice to make a paste. Rub the paste into both sides of the chops. Place the chops in a shallow dish. Pour 1 cup of the orange juice over the chops. Cover, and refrigerate for at least 8 hours or overnight, turning the chops occasionally.

2 To make the sauce, in a large, deep skillet set over high heat, add 1 tablespoon of the butter and 1 tablespoon of the oil. When the mixture is hot, add the onion and cook over medium-high heat, stirring frequently, until the onion has softened and is starting to brown, about 8 minutes. With a slotted spoon, remove the onion to a small bowl and set aside. Add the remaining 2 tablespoons of butter to the skillet over high heat. When it is hot, add the mushrooms, and cook, stirring and tossing the mushrooms, until they are lightly browned and all of the steaming has stopped. Stir in the reserved onions, the remaining 2 cups of orange juice, sherry, gravy, orange zest, and bay leaf. Remove the pork chops from the marinade and pat them dry on paper towels. Add the marinade to the sauce in the skillet. Rinse the baking dish in which the chops were marinated and set aside.

3 Over medium heat, cook the sauce, uncovered, at a brisk simmer, stirring occasionally, until it has thickened and reached a gravy-like consistency, 25 to 30 minutes. Remove from the heat and set aside.

4 Sprinkle the flour on a sheet of waxed paper and dredge the pork chops on both sides, shaking off the excess flour.

5 Preheat the oven to 325°F. Add the remaining 2 tablespoons of oil to another large skillet set over high heat. When very hot, add the pork chops and brown on both sides, adjusting the heat as necessary.

(This may have to be done in batches, adding more oil between batches.)

6 Arrange the browned chops in the baking dish. Pour the sauce over the chops. Cover the dish tightly with aluminum foil and bake for 45 to 50 minutes until the chops are fork-tender. Arrange the chops on a serving platter and spoon a little of the sauce over them. Sprinkle with chopped parsley. Serve with Ryan's Special Wild Rice, along with the remaining sauce.

Ryan's Special Wild Rice

1 cup wild rice, well rinsed in a fine-mesh strainer
1½ cups freshly squeezed orange juice
1½ cups (12 ounces) chicken broth (see page 92),
½ teaspoon salt
2 teaspoons grated orange zest
⅛ teaspoon freshly grated nutmeg
2 teaspoons orange-flavored liqueur (optional)
2 tablespoons butter, melted

1 In a large, heavy saucepan, combine the wild rice, orange juice, chicken broth, and salt. Bring to a boil, then lower the heat, cover, and simmer for 50 to 60 minutes or until the rice is tender and most of the liquid has been absorbed. Remove from the heat, and fluff with a fork. If there is any liquid left in the pan, simply drain it off. Cover tightly, and set aside for 5 minutes.

2 Stir the orange zest, nutmeg, and liqueur, if using, into the melted butter. Add the butter mixture to the hot rice, and toss until thoroughly blended.

Cabbie: **Carlos Camargo**
Country of Origin: Colombia

"Lechon"

Marinated Pork Ribs with Cuban-style Yuca

"One of the advantages of an international marriage is all of the good food that comes out of it," says Carlos. "My wife is Cuban, and these are two of her recipes that have become real favorites of mine."

It's not beautiful at all, but once beyond its homely exterior, yuca root is surprisingly tasty and easy to cook. Also known as *cassava* or *manioc*, the root is long (6 to 12 inches) and fairly thick (2 to 3 inches), with a tough, brown skin. However, when the skin is pared away, silky white flesh is revealed. The flavor is reminiscent of both a white and a sweet potato, but the texture is more fibrous than either one. Yuca can be stored in the crisper section of the refrigerator for several days.

Preparation for this recipe must be started two days before serving.

MAKES 6 TO 8 SERVINGS

3 pounds country-style pork spare ribs
1 medium-size yellow onion, coarsely chopped
 (about ½ cup)
3 cloves garlic
1½ teaspoons vegetable or olive oil
2 teaspoons kosher salt
2 teaspoons dried oregano, crumbled
½ teaspoon freshly ground black pepper
1 cup water
2 tablespoons white vinegar
Cuban-style Yuca (recipe follows), for serving

1 With a sharp knife, lightly score the meaty side of the ribs. In a mini food processor or a blender, process together the onion, garlic, oil, salt, oregano, and pepper until the mixture forms a loose paste. Rub this mixture onto all sides and between the ribs. (Depending on how the meat person cuts them, the ribs may still be attached at the backbone or they may be cut apart completely and reformed.) Place the meat on a platter or in a glass dish. Cover tightly and refrigerate for 2 days. (It is not necessary to turn the meat during this time.)

2 Preheat the oven to 400°F. Place the ribs in a shallow roasting pan or baking dish, meaty-side up. Pour the water mixed with the vinegar into the bottom of the pan. Cover tightly, and roast for 1 hour, then lower the oven temperature to 300°F and roast for another 2 hours. Remove the roasting pan from the oven. (If necessary, the ribs can be set aside for 15 or 20 minutes while completing the yuca.)

3 To serve, arrange the ribs on a serving

platter. Pour the juices that have accumulated in the roasting pan over the meat and serve with Cuban-style Yuca.

Cuban-style Yuca

2 pounds yuca root (available in Hispanic stores and
   some supermarkets)
2 large yellow onions, coarsely chopped
   (about 2 cups)
¼ cup olive oil
4 cloves garlic, minced
½ teaspoon cayenne pepper

1 Trim the ends of the yuca and cut into more manageable lengths. With a vegetable peeler, pare off the skin. Cut the yuca into even, bite-size pieces. Place the yuca and the onions in a large saucepan, and add enough lightly salted water to cover. Set the pan over high heat, and bring to a boil. Reduce the heat and simmer, covered, until the yuca is very tender, about 25 minutes.

2 While the yuca is cooking, heat the oil in a medium-size skillet over high heat. When it is hot, stir in the garlic and cook over medium heat, stirring constantly, until the garlic is lightly browned. Remove from the heat, and stir in the cayenne.

3 Drain the yuca and onions in a colander and place in a serving bowl. Drizzle the hot oil-and-garlic mixture over the yuca, and serve immediately.

TAXI TRIVIA: John Hertz, who founded the Yellow Cab Company in 1907, chose the color yellow for his cabs because he read a University of Chicago survey that claimed that yellow was the easiest color to spot.

Cabbie: **Rivka Moskovich**

Country of Origin: Israel

Other Recipes:

Roasted Eggplant Salad (see page 16)

Meat-and-Tomato-Stuffed Eggplant (see page 121)

Glazed Oranges with Mint Syrup (see page 179)

Chicken Baked with Oranges

"I love to cook," says Rivka, who routinely drives decked out in fine jewelry and designer clothing. "But I have to be careful what I eat since my cholesterol is a little high, so I often serve chicken or turkey, and not so much red meat anymore." The onion soup mix, she admits, is definitely an American touch, but the combination of chicken and oranges is very much an Israeli tradition. "They say in my country that tahini (sesame paste) lowers cholesterol, so I eat a lot of that, too. The wine I prefer is a red from Israel called Gamlaa."

To further lower the fat in this dish, you can skin most of the chicken parts before baking, or even afterward before serving. Rivka suggests serving this dish with white or brown rice, to which she adds some crisp-cooked carrot slices and peas. She also stirs in some of the sauce from the baking dish.

MAKES 4 TO 6 SERVINGS

1 (3½- to 4-pound) broiler-fryer chicken, cut into 8 parts

1 envelope Lipton dry onion soup mix (from a 2-ounce package)

½ cup freshly squeezed orange juice (about 1½ oranges)

1 navel orange, washed well, ends trimmed, cut into ¼-inch slices, and the slices cut in half

Chopped fresh parsley, for garnish

1 Place the chicken parts skin-side up in a shallow baking dish just large enough to hold them comfortably in one layer. Empty the packet of soup mix into a small bowl, and toss until well blended. Sprinkle evenly over the chicken. Cover the baking dish loosely, and refrigerate for at least 1 hour or up to 8 hours.

2 Preheat the oven to 375°F. Uncover the chicken, and pour the orange juice between the chicken pieces into the bottom of the baking dish. Arrange the orange slices over the chicken. Cover tightly with aluminum foil. Bake until the chicken is very tender, but not yet falling from the bones, about 1¼ hours.

3 To serve, sprinkle with parsley, and garnish individual servings with the cooked orange slices.

Cabbie: **Charles S. Vrazel**

Country of Origin: United States

BEING A CABBIE: "I love my work, although I've only been doing it for a year. I used to drive a long-distance truck route, but driving a cab is better. I get to go home at night to a comfortable bed and my own home cooking, which is a lot better than any truck stop."

Vrazel's Easy Chicken Casserole

"I'm a single guy, and I often invite women for dinner," says Charles. "This same recipe can be made with a brisket of beef, if you want. Whether it's chicken or beef, I serve it with egg noodles and a tossed salad or steamed asparagus, along with a good bottle of wine. For dessert, I buy a couple of slices of good New York cheesecake from a deli and serve it with coffee, along with a cordial glass of Sambuca or Frangelica. The leftovers I put away in the refrigerator and reheat for myself another night or two."

MAKES 6 SERVINGS

1 (3½- to 4-pound) broiler-fryer chicken, cut into 8 parts and each breast cut in half, crosswise

3 or 4 carrots, peeled and finely chopped (about 1½ cups)

2 ribs celery, finely chopped (about 1 cup)

10 to 12 medium-size white mushrooms, sliced (about 8 ounces)

2 (10¾-ounce) cans cream of mushroom soup

1 envelope dry onion soup mix (from a 2-ounce package)

Hot cooked egg noodles, for serving

Chopped fresh parsley, for garnish

1 Preheat the oven to 350°F. In a shallow baking dish or roasting pan, arrange the chicken pieces in one layer, skin-side up. Scatter the carrots, celery, and mushrooms over the chicken.

2 In a medium-size bowl, stir together the mushroom soup and the onion soup mix until well blended. Spoon and spread the soup mixture evenly over the chicken and vegetables. Cover the baking dish tightly with aluminum foil, and bake for 2 hours.

3 To serve, place the noodles on a large platter. Arrange the chicken pieces over the noodles. Spoon a little of the pan gravy over the chicken and noodles. Sprinkle with parsley. Serve the remaining pan gravy separately.

Cabbie: **Martin Pinchuck**

Country of Origin: United States

Meatball and Chicken Drumstick Fricassee

"I got most of the recipes I cook from my mother," Martin told us. "She was a great cook and a wonderful person. Usually she served white rice with this dish." This dish boasts such Slavic touches as meatballs, lemon juice, and even sugar.

MAKES 6 TO 8 SERVINGS

½ pound ground beef

¼ cup plain dry bread crumbs

1 small yellow onion, minced (about ¼ cup)

¼ cup chopped fresh parsley

2 tablespoons warm water

Salt and freshly ground black pepper

12 chicken wings, tips removed and discarded

6 broiler-fryer chicken drumsticks

6 tablespoons vegetable oil

1 medium-size yellow onion, chopped (about ½ cup)

2 cloves garlic, minced

1¼ cups boiling water

¼ cup sugar

¼ cup freshly squeezed lemon juice

1 tablespoon browning sauce (such as Gravy Master or Kitchen Bouquet)

Hot cooked white rice, for serving

■ In a large bowl, with your hands, gently mix together the ground beef with the bread crumbs, minced onion, parsley, warm water, ½ teaspoon salt, and ⅛ teaspoon pepper. Scoop the mixture out of the bowl by the measuring tablespoonful and roll between the palms of your hands into 18 firm balls, and set aside.

② Season the chicken pieces with salt and pepper and set aside.

③ Heat 2 tablespoons of the oil in a large Dutch oven or other heavy stew pot over high heat. When the oil is hot, add the chopped onion, and cook, stirring, over medium heat until softened, 3 to 5 minutes. Add the garlic, and cook, stirring, for about 1 minute. With a slotted spoon, remove the onion and garlic to a small bowl and set aside.

④ Add 2 more tablespoons of oil to the pot. When it is hot, add the meatballs and brown them on all sides, turning and adjusting the heat as necessary, until the balls are crisp brown and cooked through, 8 to 10 minutes. Remove with the slotted spoon to a bowl. Cover lightly and set aside.

5 Add the remaining 2 tablespoons of oil to the pot. When it is hot, add the chicken pieces and cook, turning and adjusting the heat as necessary, until golden on both sides. Tilt the pan, and spoon off and discard as much of the grease remaining in the pot as possible. Return the onion and garlic to the pot.

6 While the chicken is cooking, stir together the boiling water, sugar, lemon juice, and browning sauce until the sugar is dissolved. Pour over the chicken mixture. Cover tightly, and simmer gently for 45 minutes to 1 hour, basting occasionally, until the chicken is tender and just beginning to fall from the bones.

7 Add the meatballs, and continue to cook until they are heated through, about 5 minutes. Season to taste with salt and pepper, and serve immediately with the cooked rice.

TAXI TRIVIA: Taxi fares are computed on an electronic meter, boldly displayed in the front of the cab. There is no surcharge for the number of passengers above one, although four passengers is the maximum allowed. For quite some time now there has been a flat surcharge, which is displayed on the meter, that is charged after dark to encourage cabbies to drive at night. Tipping isn't required, of course, but it is the accepted practice, averaging between fifteen and twenty-five percent of the fare.

Cabbie: **Arshad Iqbal**

Country of Origin: Pakistan

Other Recipes:

Chapli: Pakistani Ground Beef in Pita Breads (see page 136)

Spiced Rice with Peas (see page 148)

Raita: An Indian Condiment (see page 161)

Kharathi Stewed Chicken

"I know Americans like chicken as much as we do in Pakistan. This recipe, which is very easy, is our version of chicken stew, only a lot more spicy than what you eat in this country." Arshad suggests accompanying this chicken dish with his recipe for *Raita* (see page 161) and a simple blend of white or brown rice and freshly cooked peas.

MAKES 4 TO 6 SERVINGS

2 pounds firm, ripe tomatoes, peeled, seeded, and coarsely chopped (see Note, page 122), or 2 (14½-ounce) cans diced tomatoes, drained

3 cloves garlic, minced

½-inch piece fresh ginger, peeled and minced

½ teaspoon garam masala (available in Middle Eastern markets)

¼ teaspoon salt

¼ teaspoon freshly ground black pepper

6 tablespoons vegetable oil

1 (3½- to 4-pound) broiler-fryer chicken, cut into 8 parts

Hot cooked white or brown rice, for serving

1 In a medium-size bowl, mix the tomatoes with the garlic, ginger, garam masala, salt, and pepper; set aside.

2 Heat 3 tablespoons of the oil in a large skillet set over high heat. When it is very hot, add a few pieces of the chicken, and cook, turning and adjusting the heat as necessary, until golden on both sides, about 10 minutes. Remove the chicken and set aside. Repeat with the remaining chicken pieces, adding only as much oil as necessary to promote even browning. Discard the excess oil in the skillet, but be sure to save any crusty, brown bits that cling to the bottom.

3 Return the chicken to the skillet, and spoon the tomato mixture over it. Cook, covered, over medium-low heat, basting the chicken frequently with the pan juices, until the chicken is fork-tender but not falling from the bones, 15 to 20 minutes. Serve with white or brown rice.

Cabbie: **David Ghalian**
Country of Origin: Jordan

"Meloukhiah"
Chicken with Chopped Collard Greens and Garlic

"This recipe is also popular in Egypt," David says. "The same dish can be made with okra and lamb, if you like. Use about one pound of okra and one pound of boned leg of lamb cut into big cubes. What you drink depends on if you are Christian or Muslim. Christians would drink Arak whiskey, which is made from grapes. Muslims would drink tea or coffee."

MAKES 4 TO 6 SERVINGS

1 (3½- to 4-pound) broiler-fryer chicken, cut into 8 parts, and each breast cut crosswise into 3
1 small yellow onion, cut into thin slices and the slices separated into rings
2 cups (16 ounces) chicken broth (see page 92)
1 pound collard greens
¼ cup extra-virgin olive oil
4 cloves garlic, thinly sliced crosswise

1 Place the chicken pieces in a large Dutch oven or other heavy stew pot and scatter the onion rings on top. Add the chicken broth and bring to a boil. Lower the heat, cover tightly, and simmer slowly for 30 to 40 minutes, or until the chicken is fork-tender, but not yet starting to fall from the bones.

2 While the chicken is cooking, cut the tough veins from the center of each collard leaf, and discard. Wash the leaves in several changes of cold water and drain. Chop the greens coarsely and set aside.

3 With tongs, remove the chicken pieces from the pot to a bowl. Cover and keep warm. Stir the chopped collard greens into the broth. Bring to a boil, then lower the heat, cover, and boil slowly for 15 minutes.

4 While the greens are cooking, heat the olive oil with the garlic in a small saucepan over medium-low heat. Simmer until the garlic is tender and lightly browned, about 10 minutes.

5 Drain the collard greens into a colander, then return the greens to the cooking pot. Add the warm oil-and-garlic mixture, and toss until well blended. Place the greens on a large platter. Arrange the chicken pieces on top of the greens and serve immediately.

Cabbie: **Jaafar Elmehdi**

Country of Origin: Morocco

Other Recipes:

Tagine: Fish Baked with Olives, Parsley, and Garlic (see page 81)

"Bastela"

Moroccan Phyllo and Chicken Pie

"Americans might find the sugar-and-spice mixture on top of this pie very strange," says Jaafar. "I was once describing it to a lady I was driving and she said, 'Oh, like a sugar-cookie topping . . . but with *chicken*?' I explained to her that this topping is most traditional and she should try it. With this we would serve hot Mint Tea (see page 50)."

MAKES 6 SERVINGS

1 (3½- to 4-pound) broiler-fryer chicken, cut into 8 parts

2 medium-size yellow onions, cut into large pieces

1 bunch fresh parsley, tender stems and leaves chopped separately

1¼ teaspoons salt

½ teaspoon freshly ground black pepper

6 ounces (1½ sticks) butter

1 cup (4 ounces) slivered blanched almonds

2 tablespoons sesame seeds

1 teaspoon ground cumin

1 teaspoon paprika

½ teaspoon ground cinnamon

1 large yellow onion, chopped (about 1 cup)

14 sheets (½ pound) phyllo dough (see How to Handle Phyllo Dough, page 31)

¼ cup confectioners' sugar

Pinch freshly grated nutmeg

1 Place the chicken pieces in a large soup pot. Add the onion chunks, parsley stems, 1 teaspoon of the salt, and ¼ teaspoon of the pepper. Add enough water to cover the chicken. Bring to a boil over high heat. Reduce the heat, cover, and simmer until the chicken is ready to fall from the bones, about 45 minutes.

2 With tongs or a slotted spoon, remove the chicken pieces from the pot to a bowl and set aside. Strain the broth through a sieve into a bowl. Measure out ½ cup of the broth and set aside. Reserve the remaining broth for another use.

3 Heat 6 tablespoons of the butter in a large skillet. When it is hot, add the almonds and cook over medium heat, stirring, until they are golden, 2 to 3 minutes. With a slotted spoon, remove the almonds to a small bowl and set aside.

4 To the skillet, add the sesame seeds, cumin, paprika, and cinnamon. Cook, stirring, for about 30 seconds until the spices are fragrant. Reduce the heat to medium-low and stir in the chopped onion. Cook, stirring frequently, until the onion is softened, 3 to 5 minutes. Remove from the heat and stir in the reserved ½ cup of chicken broth, chopped parsley leaves, the remaining ¼ teaspoon of salt, and remaining ¼ teaspoon of pepper.

5 Remove the chicken meat from the bones. Discard the skin and bones, and cut the meat into small pieces. Stir the chicken into the onion mixture and set aside.

6 Preheat the oven to 425°F. Coat a 13 x 9-inch baking pan with vegetable cooking spray. In a small saucepan, melt the remaining 6 tablespoons of butter and set aside.

7 Arrange 6 sheets of the phyllo dough crosswise across the baking pan so that half of each sheet covers the bottom and a quarter of the sheet hangs over each side of the pan. Brush the top sheet with melted butter. Spoon half the chicken mixture evenly into the pan, then sprinkle with half the reserved almonds. Top with 4 more sheets of phyllo as before, brushing the top sheet with butter. Spoon the remaining chicken mixture into the pan. Bring up the edges of the phyllo that are hanging over the sides of the pan and fold them over the chicken mixture to enclose it. On a work surface, lightly butter one sheet of the remaining phyllo. Top with 3 more sheets of phyllo, brushing each one with butter. Place the stack of buttered sheets lengthwise on the pie and, using a pancake turner, neatly tuck in the edges around the inside rim of the pan. Brush with the remaining butter.

8 Place the pan in the oven, and bake for 10 minutes. Meanwhile, finely chop the remaining almonds and set aside. In a small bowl, combine the confectioners' sugar and nutmeg. Place the sugar mixture in a small, fine-mesh sieve and set aside.

9 Remove the pan from the oven. Place a jelly-roll pan upside down over the top of the baking pan. Carefully flip the two pans over to turn the pie out of the baking pan and onto the jelly-roll pan. Shake the sieve containing the sugar mixture evenly over the pie. Return to the oven, and bake for 5 minutes. Sprinkle the chopped almonds over the pie, and continue to bake for 3 to 5 minutes, or until the pie is golden and crisp. Set aside for about 10 minutes.

10 To serve, cut into slices with a very long, sharp knife.

BIG APPLE BITE: The downtown-Manhattan neighborhood SoHo stands for South of Houston Street.

Cabbie: **Matin Chowdhury**

Country of Origin: Bangladesh

Kowshar's Tandoori Chicken

Matin says there are many versions of this famous dish, which is usually made with chicken, but also with red meat. However, the one thing all *tandoor* recipes have in common is that they are cooked in a *tandoor*, a tall, cylindrical oven made of brick and clay, in which is built a very hot wood-and-charcoal fire. In fact, the fire is so hot that a whole chicken cooks in just a few minutes. Western cooks can more or less duplicate this method by using a hooded charcoal grill and a very hot fire.

"This is my wife, Kowshar's, recipe. She serves it warm with pita bread and *Raita* (see page 161) and usually some sliced onion and wedges of tomato. Other times she makes basmati rice mixed with peas. Our American friends also seem to enjoy eating mango chutney with tandoori."

Preparation for this recipe must be started at least 8 hours or the day before serving.

MAKES 4 SERVINGS

4 broiler-fryer chicken legs (drumsticks and thighs, 3 to 4 pounds total weight)

1 cup plain yogurt

2 tablespoons sour cream

1 small yellow onion, shredded (about ¼ cup)

2 small cloves garlic, minced

2 tablespoons garam masala (available in Middle Eastern markets)

1 teaspoon ground cumin

½ teaspoon ground ginger

2 tablespoons butter, melted

Hot cooked basmati rice (see page 149), for serving

Cilantro sprigs, for garnish

1 Cut the drumsticks and thighs apart, then pull off the skin and discard. To keep a firm hold on the skin, use paper towels to help you get a grip, then gently pull the skin off the meat. With a sharp knife, make three or four shallow gashes in the top of each of the chicken pieces.

2 In a large bowl, stir together the yogurt, sour cream, onion, garlic, garam masala, cumin, and ginger until well blended. Rub this mixture onto each chicken piece, making sure it gets well into the gashes. Place the chicken pieces in the remaining yogurt mixture. Cover, and marinate in the refrigerator for at least 8 hours or overnight, turning occasionally.

3 Position a rack in the center of the oven. Preheat the oven to 450°F. Set a wire rack large enough to hold all the chicken pieces in one layer in the bottom of a roasting pan or baking dish. Arrange the chicken on the rack. Place in the oven, and roast for 5 minutes. Turn, and roast on the other side for 5 minutes. Turn again, and brush with the melted butter. Raise the oven temperature to 500°F. Continue to roast for about 10 minutes, or until the chicken is golden brown and the juices run clear when the tip of a knife is inserted into the thighs.

4 To serve, arrange the chicken on a serving platter surrounding the rice. Garnish with sprigs of cilantro.

BIG APPLE BITE: In 1978, the first annual Empire State Building Run-Up was inaugurated with the help of the New York Road Runners Club. Fifteen runners ran up 1,575 steps from the lobby to the 86th floor.

Chapter 3 Appetizers and First Courses Meat and Poultry Fish and Seafood Hearty Soups and Stews Casseroles and Skillet Meals Side Dishes and Salads Breads and Baked Goods Desserts and Other Sweet Things Appetizers and First Courses Meat and Poultry Fish and Seafood Hearty Soups and Stews Casseroles and Skillet Meals Side Dishes and Salads Breads and Baked Goods Desserts and Other Sweet Things Appetizers and First Courses Meat and Poultry Fish and Seafood Hearty Soups and Stews Casseroles and Skillet Meals Side Dishes and Salads Breads and Baked Goods Desserts Other Sweet Things Appetizers and First Courses Meat and Poultry Fish and Seafood Hearty Soups and Stews Casseroles and Skillet Meals Side Dishes and Salads Breads and Baked Goods Desserts and Other Sweet Things Appetizers and First Courses Meat and Poultry Fish and Seafood Hearty Soups and Stews Casseroles and Skillet Meals Side Dishes and Salads Breads and Baked Goods Desserts and Other Sweet Things Appetizers and First Courses Meat and Poultry Fish and Seafood Hearty Soups and Stews Casseroles and Skillet Meals Side Dishes and Salads Breads Baked Goods Desserts and Other Sweet Things Appetizers and First Courses Meat and Poultry Fish and Seafood Hearty Soups and Stews Casseroles and Skillet Meals Side Dishes and Salads Breads Baked Goods Desserts and Other Sweet Things Appetizers and First Courses Meat and Poultry Fish and Seafood Hearty Soups and Stews Casseroles and Skillet Meals Side Dishes and Salads Breads and Baked Goods Desserts and Other Sweet Things Appetizers and First Courses Meat and Poultry Fish and Seafood Hearty Soups and Stews Casseroles and Skillet Meals Side Dishes and Salads Breads and Baked Goods Desserts and Other Sweet Things Appetizers and First Courses Meat and Poultry Fish and Seafood Hearty Soups and Stews Casseroles and Skillet Meals Side Dishes Salads Breads and Baked Goods Desserts and Other Sweet Things Appetizers and First Courses Meat and Poultry Fish and Seafood Hearty Soups and Stews Casseroles and Skillet Meals Side Dishes and Salads Breads and Baked Goods Desserts and Other Sweet Things Appetizers and First Courses Meat and Poultry Fish and Seafood Hearty Soups and Stews Casseroles and Skillet Meals Side Dishes and Salads Breads and Baked Goods Desserts and Other Sweet Things Appetizers and First Courses Meat and Poultry Fish and Seafood Hearty Soups and Stews Casseroles and Skillet Meals Side Dishes and Salads Breads and Baked Goods Desserts and Other Sweet Things Appetizers and First Courses Meat and Poultry Fish and Seafood Hearty Soups and Stews Casseroles and Skillet Meals Side Dishes and Salads Breads and Baked Goods Desserts and Other Sweet Things Appetizers and First Courses Meat and Poultry Fish and Seafood Hearty Soups and Stews Casseroles and Skillet Meals Side Dishes and Salads Breads and Baked Goods Desserts and Other Sweet Things

TAXI TRIVIA: The average mileage on a retiring taxicab is 250,000, but very often more, up to 300,000 miles.

Cabbie: **Alex Wong**

Country of Origin: Hong Kong

A Whole Steamed Fish

"Americans should not be afraid to cook a whole fish," says Alex. "It's easy, and we Asians like whole fish, especially fish heads, even though we know that most Americans don't." Alex says he serves the fish with steamed white rice and lightly steamed broccoli or asparagus, which he seasons with either a few drops of Asian sesame oil or fresh lemon juice.

Since most Americans don't own a fish poacher (a long, lidded pot with a rack that is designed to accommodate a whole fish), you may have to improvise one in order to cook the fish properly. Use a small, shallow baking pan and place a rack (such as a wire cooling rack) in the bottom. Cover the pan tightly with a piece of heavy-duty aluminum foil.

Obtaining a whole fish is sometimes difficult. It's possible to improvise with two skin-on fish fillets, which can be steamed together, flesh sides facing, thus simulating a whole fish.

MAKES 4 SERVINGS

1 whole fish (it really doesn't matter which kind, as long as it's the right size and you like it), weighing about 2 pounds, cleaned and gutted, but with the tail left on, or 2 skin-on fillets, each weighing about ¾ pound

1 large bunch parsley (separate the coarse stems, reserve a few sprigs to chop for garnish, and save the remainder for another use)

6 to 8 scallions (separate dark green tops, and slice the remaining white and light green parts)

2 cloves garlic, minced

1-inch piece fresh ginger, shredded (discard the stringy pieces that collect on the outside of the grater)

2 tablespoons Japanese soy sauce

1 tablespoon peanut oil

1 tablespoon rice wine vinegar

1 teaspoon honey

½ teaspoon Asian sesame oil

Hot cooked white rice, cooked according to package, for serving

Steamed broccoli or asparagus, for serving

1 Remove the rack from a fish poacher or baking pan. Add about 1 inch of water to the pan. (The water should not reach the level of the rack. If the rack is too low in the pan, invert two custard cups in the pan on which to set the rack.)

2 Rinse the fish inside and out, and pat dry with paper towels. With a sharp knife, make several shallow, diagonal slashes across one side of the whole fish (or on the skin side of one of the fillets); set aside. Arrange the parsley stems and scallion tops on the rack. (Aside from adding flavor, the parsley and scallion tops will prevent the fish from sticking to the rack.)

3 To make the sauce, in a small bowl, mix together the garlic, ginger, soy sauce, peanut oil, rice wine vinegar, honey, and sesame oil. Brush the inside and the top of the fish with the sauce, making sure to brush it onto the flesh exposed by the slashes. (If using fillets, brush the flesh side of each fillet with the garlic, and use the slashed fillet on top.) Reserve the remaining sauce. Place the fish on the prepared rack, slashed-side up. Sprinkle with the sliced scallions.

▣ Set the poacher over two burners and bring the water to a boil. Lower the rack into the pan of boiling water. Cover the pan tightly, with aluminum foil if necessary. Reduce the heat slightly and steam for 10 to 15 minutes, or just until the slashes in the skin have spread apart and the flesh is opaque. You might also want to check carefully the inside of the fish or between the fillets. Remove the rack from the pan. Place the fish on a platter, leaving the parsley stems and scallion tops on the rack to be discarded. Cover the platter with aluminum foil, and place it in a warm (170°F) oven. Add the reserved sauce to the liquid left in the pan, and bring to a boil. Boil hard for about 10 minutes, or until the liquid is reduced by at least half to make a thin sauce.

▣ To serve, spoon the sauce over the fish and sprinkle with chopped parsley. Serve with white or brown rice and steamed broccoli or asparagus.

BIG APPLE BITE: Approximately half a million visitors gather in chilly Times Square every New Years Eve to watch the ball drop.

Cabbie: **Elsayed M. Ramadam**
Country of Origin: Egypt

Other Recipes:

Fasolia: Beef and Green Bean Casserole (see page 123)

White Beans with Zucchini (see page 153)

Middle Eastern Chopped Salad with Tahini Dressing (see page 162)

"Samak Magly"
Fried Porgy

"Almost all of the fish we eat in Egypt are porgies," Elsayed tells us. "These are small fish with a mild flavor, but you can use any small fish you like, even trout. We leave the tails on, since the tails, when they are fried crisp, are a delicacy. We view this unusual way of preparing small fish as the Middle Eastern version of Cajun blackening. However, don't leave the rubs on for too long, since the delicate fish flesh will absorb these flavors more readily than either meat or poultry. I serve the fish with my Middle Eastern Chopped Salad (see page 162), but for this I use an oil-and-vinegar dressing instead of Tahini Dressing (see page162).

MAKES 4 SERVINGS

Inside Rub

4 cloves garlic, minced

1 teaspoon salt

1 teaspoon ground cumin

½ teaspoon freshly ground black pepper

1 tablespoon water

Outside Rub

1 clove garlic, minced

½ teaspoon salt

½ teaspoon ground cardamom

⅛ teaspoon freshly ground black pepper

1 tablespoon freshly squeezed lemon juice

Fish

4 porgies or other small fish, about 8 ounces
  each, cleaned and gutted

½ cup all-purpose flour

¼ cup vegetable oil

Chopped fresh parsley, for garnish

Lemon wedges

1 Prepare the Inside Rub for the fish: In a small bowl, mix together the garlic, salt, cumin, pepper, and water until the mixture forms a thin paste, and set aside.

2 Prepare the Outside Rub for the fish: In a small bowl, mix together the garlic, salt, cardamom, and pepper. Add the lemon juice, and stir to make a thin paste.

3 Prepare the Fish: Rinse the fish under cold running water, and pat dry inside and out with paper towels. Spread the Inside Rub in each fish. Spread each fish with the Outside Rub. Set the fish aside for 30 minutes to absorb the rubs. (Any longer than this and the fish should be refrigerated.)

4 Sprinkle the flour on a sheet of waxed paper. Dredge both sides of each fish generously in the flour.

5 Heat the oil in a large skillet over medium-high heat. When it is hot, add the fish, and cook until browned on each side and the flesh flakes when lightly touched with a fork, 3 to 4 minutes per side. This will probably have to be done in two batches. Keep the first batch of fish in a warm (170°F) oven while frying the second batch. Sprinkle the fish with parsley and serve with lemon wedges.

BIG APPLE BITE: The suspension of four giant cables, each three feet in diameter, holds the George Washington Bridge in place. The cables contain 26,424 wires, each thinner than a pencil. Stretched out, the wires would reach 107,000 miles—nearly halfway to the moon.

Cabbie: **Dennis Launer**

Country of Origin: United States

Other Recipes:

Stuffed Cabbage in Sweet Tomato Sauce (see page 114)

Gingered New Potatoes (see page 146)

Steamed Bok Choy (see page 154)

PROFILE: "I used to work in restaurants, first waiting tables, then cooking, which I've always enjoyed, but there wasn't enough money in that business, and that's why I started driving a cab. I learned quite a lot about cooking and food while I was working with some very talented chefs. It inspired me to invent some of my own recipes. Nowadays, friends always ask me why I don't open a restaurant of my own. But do you have any idea how much that would cost? Well, maybe I'll win the lottery."

Pan-Broiled Mako Shark (or Swordfish) Steaks

Shark steaks, particularly mako shark, are becoming more commonplace, but swordfish steaks can always be used instead with excellent results. In this recipe, Dennis puts an Asian spin on the fish, as well as on the accompaniments of Gingered New Potatoes and Steamed Bok Choy, both of which he created especially for this entree.

MAKES 4 SERVINGS

4 mako shark or swordfish steaks, ¾ to 1 inch thick and 6 to 8 ounces each

½ cup Worcestershire sauce

2 tablespoons chopped cilantro

2 tablespoons minced shallots

1 clove garlic, minced

Freshly ground black pepper

2 tablespoons butter

2 tablespoons vegetable or olive oil

Chopped fresh parsley, for garnish

Gingered New Potatoes (see page 146), for serving

Steamed Bok Choy (see page 154), for serving

1 Rinse the fish and pat dry. In a shallow, glass baking dish, mix together the Worcestershire sauce, cilantro, shallots, garlic, and pepper. Lay the steaks in the marinade, and turn to coat. Cover, and refrigerate for 2 or 3 hours, turning the fish once or twice.

2 Heat the butter and oil together in a large skillet over high heat. When the oil and butter are very hot, remove the steaks from the baking dish, reserving the marinade, and place the steaks in the skillet. Cook over medium heat, turning once, until nicely browned and the interiors are opaque, 3 to 4 minutes on each side. Be careful not to overcook, or the fish will be dry.

3 Remove the fish to dinner plates. Add the reserved marinade to the hot skillet, and cook, stirring, until bubbling hot and slightly thickened. Spoon a little of the sauce over each fish steak, sprinkle with parsley, and serve immediately with Gingered New Potatoes and Steamed Bok Choy.

Cabbie: **Jaafar Elmehdi**
Country of Origin: Morocco

Other Recipes:

Bastela: Moroccan Phyllo and Chicken Pie (see page 70)

PROFILE: "Presently I am studying electrical engineering at City College. Driving a cab is just temporary for me. Just a good way to make a living while I go to school. Also, I meet many nice people who encourage me to continue my education."

"Tagine"

Fish Baked with Olives, Parsley, and Garlic

"The word *tagine* means two different things," says Jaafar, "either a traditional stew of meat, poultry, or fish, or a conical-shaped, earthenware vessel in which we cook it." Although tagines can be purchased in many better kitchenware stores, it's safe to say that most American kitchens do not contain one. An ordinary baking dish is an acceptable substitute if it is *very tightly* covered. Tagines are almost always served with couscous, which is the "rice" or "pasta" of Morocco, Jaafar tells us.

MAKES 4 SERVINGS

¼ cup extra-virgin olive oil

1 medium-size yellow onion, very finely chopped
  (about ½ cup)

3 cloves garlic, minced

1 cup finely chopped fresh parsley

Freshly ground black pepper

4 flounder or sole fillets, each weighing about
  6 ounces

½ pound (drained weight) pitted Middle Eastern
  green olives (see Note), coarsely chopped
  (about 2 cups)

1 lemon, very thinly sliced

Paprika, to taste

Couscous, cooked according to package directions,
  for serving

1 Preheat the oven to 400°F. Use a small amount of the olive oil to grease a shallow baking dish that is just large enough to hold the stuffed fillets in one layer, and set aside.

2 Heat 1 tablespoon of the remaining olive oil in a medium-size skillet over medium heat. When it is hot, add the onion and garlic, and cook, stirring, just until the onion is softened, 3 to 5 minutes. Remove from the heat and stir in the parsley and pepper, and set aside.

3 Rinse the fillets and pat dry with paper towels. Lay the fillets out flat on a work surface, inside up. Spread the onion mixture down the center of each fillet, dividing evenly. Fold the fillet over the onion mixure, and secure with a couple of toothpicks. Arrange the stuffed fillets in the prepared baking dish. Spoon the chopped olives evenly over the fillets. Arrange the lemon slices over the olives. Drizzle evenly with the remaining olive oil, then sprinkle lightly with paprika.

4 Cover the baking dish *very tightly* with aluminum foil, and bake for 20 minutes. Remove the foil, and test the fish for doneness. It should flake when lightly touched with a fork. Serve immediately, accompanied by hot couscous.

NOTE: The Easy Way to Pit Olives—If you can find good pitted olives, by all means use them. Otherwise, don't hesitate to pit them yourself. It isn't difficult. Lay the olive on its side, then press down on the olive with the flat side of a large, heavy knife. This splits the olive, and the pit will slip out easily.

BIG APPLE BITE: After a forty-four-year drought, the "Subway Series" returned to New York in 2000, and Yankees fans celebrated a 4–1 victory over the Mets.

Cabbie: **Claudio Paula**

Country of Origin: Dominican Republic

Steamed Fish and Vegetables with Garlic Butter

"There is quite a lot of Spanish influence on our part of the island," Claudio tells us, "and this recipe is a good example of the sophisticated cooking in Madrid. I would recommend a nice rosé wine with this healthy dish. I would also suggest flan (Spanish custard) for dessert, or a variety of cut fruit."

Our tasters rated this dish triple-A. Even those who readily admitted that fish was not one of their particular favorites asked for seconds. We think it's the onion-and-garlic sauce that really does the trick. To make things go more quickly, you can buy most of the vegetables called for in this recipe, ready to cook, at the supermarket.

MAKES 6 SERVINGS

1 cup trimmed and cut green beans

1 cup peeled baby carrots, cut in half lengthwise

1 cup trimmed and cut asparagus spears

1 cup red or yellow bell pepper strips

1 cup broccoli florets

1 cup cauliflower florets

Salt and freshly ground black pepper, to taste

6 fish fillets, such as flounder, cod, or snapper, about 6 ounces each

4 tablespoons extra-virgin olive oil

1 medium-size yellow onion, chopped (about ½ cup)

3 cloves garlic, minced

4 tablespoons (½ stick) butter

½ cup chopped fresh parsley

1 Preheat the oven to 350°F. Butter a 13 x 9-inch baking dish and set aside.

2 Bring a large pot of water to a boil. Plunge the green beans, carrots, asparagus, bell pepper strips, broccoli florets, and cauliflower florets into the boiling water. When the water returns to a boil, cook until the vegetables are fork tender, 3 to 4 minutes. Drain in a colander and rinse with cold water to preserve the color and stop further cooking. Turn the vegetables into the prepared baking dish, smoothing them to make an even layer. Season lightly with salt and pepper.

3 Rinse the fish fillets. Arrange the fillets over the vegetables in one layer. Season lightly with salt and pepper. Cover the baking dish tightly with aluminum foil. Bake for 25 to 30 minutes, or until the fish flakes when lightly touched with a fork.

3 While the fish is baking, in a large skillet, heat 2 tablespoons of the oil over high heat. When it is hot, add the onion, and cook over medium heat, stirring frequently, until very soft and just starting to brown, about 8 minutes. Stir in the garlic,

and cook briefly until softened, about 1 minute. Stir in the butter and the remaining 2 tablespoons of olive oil. Continue to cook and stir until the butter and oil are very hot. Stir in the parsley until well blended.

4 Remove the fish from the oven. Spoon the hot onion mixture evenly over the fillets and vegetables, and serve immediately.

Cabbie: **Joaquin Montes**
Country of Origin: Spain

"Marescada"
Steamed Clams, Mussels, Shrimp, and Scallops

"A friend of mine, a chef at a Spanish restaurant, gave me this recipe," says this cabbie who has been in the United States for thirty years and driving a cab for seven of them. "I often serve this when I invite friends to dinner, since it goes together quickly, and I don't have a lot of time to spend cooking when I have driven for twelve hours that day. I usually serve my *marescada* preceded by a salad of thinly sliced tomatoes, sweet onion, carrots, and celery with a simple oil-and-vinegar dressing. And, of course, a good loaf of bread. A dry white wine, I think, is the best accompaniment."

MAKES 4 TO 6 SERVINGS

24 tightly closed small mussels, scrubbed
12 tightly closed littleneck clams, scrubbed
6 cups water
½ pound large unpeeled shrimp, rinsed
½ pound sea scallops, rinsed
¼ cup extra-virgin olive oil
3 cloves garlic, minced
2 tablespoons all-purpose flour
½ cup dry white wine
  or dry vermouth
Salt, to taste
3 tablespoons chopped fresh parsley
Hot cooked white rice, for serving

1 With a paring knife, scrape away the beards from the mussels (although in this day of cultivated mussels, much debearding is rarely necessary), then rinse under cold water. Place the mussels and clams together in a large bowl, and add plenty of cold water to cover. Set aside for about 30 minutes to 1 hour, swishing the mussels and clams in the water with your hand now and then. Drain in a colander and rinse under cold, running water.

2 Place the clams and the 6 cups of water in a Dutch oven or other large, heavy saucepan set over high heat, and bring to a slow boil. Lower the heat and simmer

until the clams open, stirring with a heavy, wooden spoon (to prevent breaking the shells). With a slotted spoon, remove the clams to a large bowl, discarding any that have not opened. Add the mussels to the simmering liquid, and cook, stirring with the wooden spoon, until the shells open. With the slotted spoon, transfer the mussels to the bowl containing the clams, discarding any that have not opened. Drop the shrimp into the simmering liquid, and cook just until they turn bright pink, 1 to 2 minutes. With the slotted spoon, transfer the shrimp to the bowl. Add the scallops to the pan, and cook just until they are firm and opaque, 2 to 3 minutes. Transfer the scallops to the bowl. Cover the bowl and set aside. Ladle 3½ cups of the cooking liquid into another bowl. Discard the remaining liquid, along with any sand or other sediment, then rinse the pan and dry it.

3 Set the pan over high heat. Add the olive oil, and when it is hot, stir in the garlic. Cook over medium heat, stirring constantly, just until the garlic is softened and starting to turn golden, 1 to 2 minutes. Sprinkle the flour over the garlic, and stir until blended. Gradually add the reserved cooking liquid, stirring constantly while bringing to a boil. Boil gently for about 5 minutes, stirring occasionally. Stir in the wine, and cook for 1 minute. Season with salt, then stir in the parsley. Return the reserved seafood to the pan, stirring gently with the wooden spoon until everything is well combined and heated through. Serve over rice in warm, shallow bowls, distributing the seafood varieties as evenly as possible.

BIG APPLE BITE: On its first day of operation in 1937, 55,523 vehicles, 33,540 pedestrians, and a horse named "Rubio" crossed the George Washington Bridge. It remains one of the busiest bridges in the world, accommodating nearly 100 million vehicles each year.

Cabbie: **Joseph Bernard**

Country of Origin: France

Other Recipes:

French Vegetable-Beef Soup (see page 90)

Sausage and Apples, Normandy Style (see page 135)

Baked Shrimp à la Française

Joseph, who speaks with a charming accent, is obviously proud of the cuisine of his native country, and is eager to share his recipes. "Brittany faces the Atlantic and the Channel, and so we eat a lot of fish, and we like shrimp—*crevettes*—especially." This presentation of pink shrimp and lightly browned bread crumbs sizzling in butter is simple and unpretentious French country cooking at its best, and at the same time elegant enough to hold its own at a dinner party. Preparation time is quick, about 35 minutes from start to serving. Joseph's suggestions for accompaniments are "French bread, of course" and a "beautiful mixed salad" made with chopped, garden-fresh lettuce, diced tomatoes, bell peppers ("but not green ones; they are not really ripe, you know, and we French think they taste slightly bitter"), along with some snipped parsley, chives, and dill. Toss with Basic Vinaigrette (see page 19) "two seconds" before serving.

MAKES 4 SERVINGS

1 pound jumbo shrimp (about 16), peeled and deveined
3 slices firm white bread, slightly dried
2 tablespoons minced shallots
2 tablespoons minced fresh parsley
4 tablespoons melted butter
2 tablespoons freshly squeezed lemon juice

Preheat the oven to 375°F. Arrange the shrimp in one layer in a buttered, 1½- to 2-quart baking dish. Trim the crusts from the bread. Tear the bread into small pieces, and place in a blender or mini food processor. Blend briefly to make about 1 cup of crumbs.

2 In a small bowl, combine the bread crumbs, shallots, parsley, and 2 tablespoons of the melted butter. Stir the lemon juice into the remaining butter, and spoon evenly over the shrimp. Sprinkle the shrimp with the bread-crumb mixture, making sure that each shrimp is evenly covered. Bake for about 20 minutes, or until the crumbs are lightly browned and the shrimp are pink and firm. Serve directly from the baking dish, making sure that each serving of shrimp is coated with the bread crumb topping.

Cabbie: **Hristos Soulantzos**

Country of Origin: Greece

Other Recipes:

Crusty Country Bread (see page 168)

PROFILE: A former restaurant cook, Hristos has been driving a cab for nearly ten years, but he still draws on his professional cooking background when he prepares meals for his family and friends.

Greek-style Shrimp Scampi

Although scampi is generally thought of as an Italian presentation, the Greeks have been putting their distinctive spin on it for generations by substituting ouzo, the famous licorice-flavored Greek distillation, for the more familiar white wine or dry vermouth. Hristos, a former restaurant cook, suggests that in the true style of Greek home cooking you may want to stir a little chopped tomato into the skillet just before adding the ouzo. The scampi can also be served over orzo, the tiny rice-shaped pasta that the Greeks so dearly love.

MAKES 4 TO 6 SERVINGS

2 tablespoons butter

2 tablespoons extra-virgin olive oil

4 cloves garlic, minced

¼ teaspoon crushed red pepper, or to taste

1 pound small to medium-size shrimp, peeled and deveined (leave the tails on, if you like, for an attractive presentation)

¼ cup ouzo, dry white wine, or dry vermouth

2 tablespoons freshly squeezed lemon juice

½ cup crumbled feta cheese

¼ cup chopped fresh parsley, for garnish

Crusty Country Bread (see page 168), for serving

1 In a large skillet over high heat, stir together the butter, olive oil, garlic, and crushed red pepper, and cook just until the garlic begins to soften, about 1 minute. Add the shrimp and continue to cook over high heat, stirring and tossing, just until the shrimp turn pink, 2 to 3 minutes. Stir in the ouzo and lemon juice, and simmer for 1 minute, or just long enough for the alcohol in the wine to evaporate.

2 Transfer the shrimp and pan juices to a platter, and sprinkle with the feta and parsley. Serve immediately with Crusty Country Bread.

Chapter 4 Appetizers and First Courses Meat and Poultry Fish and Seafood Hearty Soups and Stews Casseroles and Skillet Meals Side Dishes and Salads Breads and Baked Goods Desserts and Other Sweet Things Appetizers and First Courses Meat and Poultry Fish and Seafood Hearty Soups and Stews Casseroles and Skillet Meals Side Dishes and Salads Breads and Baked Goods Desserts and Other Sweet Things Appetizers and First Courses Meat and Poultry Fish and Seafood Hearty Soups and Stews Casseroles and Skillet Meals Side Dishes and Salads Breads and Baked Goods Desserts Other Sweet Things Appetizers and First Courses Meat and Poultry Fish and Seafood Hearty Soups and Stews Casseroles and Skillet Meals Side Dishes and Salads Breads and Baked Goods Desserts and Other Sweet Things Appetizers and First Courses Meat and Poultry Fish and Seafood Hearty Soups and Stews Casseroles and Skillet Meals Side Dishes and Salads Breads and Baked Goods Desserts and Other Sweet Things Appetizers and First Courses Meat and Poultry Fish and Seafood Hearty Soups and Stews Casseroles and Skillet Meals Side Dishes and Salads Breads and Baked Goods Desserts and Other Sweet Things Appetizers and First Courses Meat and Poultry Fish and Seafood **Hearty Soups and Stews** Casseroles and Skillet Meals Side Dishes and Salads Breads and Baked Goods Desserts and Other Sweet Things Appetizers and First Courses Meat and Poultry Fish and Seafood Hearty Soups and Stews Casseroles and Skillet Meals Side Dishes and Salads Breads and Baked Goods Desserts and Other Sweet Things Appetizers and First Courses Meat and Poultry Fish and Seafood Hearty Soups and Stews Casseroles and Skillet Meals Side Dishes Salads Breads and Baked Goods Desserts and Other Sweet Things Appetizers and First Courses Meat Poultry Fish and Seafood Hearty Soups and Stews Casseroles and Skillet Meals Side Dishes and Salads Breads and Baked Goods Desserts and Other Sweet Things Appetizers and First Courses Meat and Poultry Fish and Seafood Hearty Soups and Stews Casseroles and Skillet Meals Side Dishes and Salads Breads and Baked Goods Desserts and Other Sweet Things Appetizers and First Courses Meat and Poultry Fish and Seafood Hearty Soups and Stews Casseroles and Skillet Meals Side Dishes and Salads Breads and Baked Goods Desserts and Other Sweet Things Appetizers and First Courses Meat and Poultry Fish and Seafood Hearty Soups and Stews Casseroles and Skillet Meals Side Dishes and Salads Breads and Baked Goods Desserts and Other Sweet Things Appetizers and First Courses Meat and Poultry Fish and Seafood Hearty Soups and Stews Casseroles and Skillet Meals Side Dishes and Salads Breads and Baked Goods Desserts and Other Sweet Things Appetizers and First Courses Meat and Poultry Fish and Seafood Hearty Soups and Stews Casseroles and Skillet Meals Side Dishes and Salads Breads and Baked Goods Desserts and Other Sweet Things Appetizers and First Courses Meat and Poultry Fish and Seafood Hearty Soups and Stews Casseroles Skillet Meals Side Dishes and Salads Breads and Baked Goods Desserts and Other Sweet Things

TAXI TRIVIA: NYC Cabbies hail from eighty-five different countries.

Cabbie: **Joseph Bernard**

Country of Origin: France

Other Recipes:

Baked Shrimp à la Française (see page 86)

Sausage and Apples, Normandy Style (see page 135)

French Vegetable-Beef Soup

In Brittany, it is not the custom to serve this soup upon completion. "French families cook a big pot and then serve the soup throughout the week," explains Joseph. "A good thing we do in Brittany is to take some stale French bread, slice it thinly, and float it on top of the bowls of soup. It will become moist and flavorful, as well as giving the soup a little more body."

This is a great soup on either side of the Atlantic. It's also very accommodating, depending on such things as what root vegetables are currently stashed in your refrigerator or what's available. No rutabagas at the store? No problem. Use turnips, which taste very similar. Celery ready to go limp? Go ahead and add it. Both the vegetable measurements and the varieties given here are intended only as a guide. Even the cutting and slicing needn't be precise.

MAKES 8 TO 10 SERVINGS

2 or 3 pieces cross-cut beef shank (about 2 pounds)

1½ pounds beef marrow bones

1 cup boiling water

½ head Savoy cabbage (the dark green crinkled variety), cored and thickly shredded

3 leeks, white parts only, thinly sliced and rinsed well

3 carrots, thinly sliced

2 medium-size turnips, finely chopped

1 medium-size rutabaga, finely chopped

4 cloves garlic, cut in half

1 cup chopped fresh parsley

1 tablespoon chopped fresh dill

4 cups beef broth (see page 92)

10 cups cold water

1 tablespoon salt

½ teaspoon freshly ground black pepper

1 Preheat the oven to 400°F. Cut the bones out of the beef shanks and set them aside. Cut each piece of meat into 2 or 3 large chunks, and refrigerate. Place the beef bones, including the shank bones, in a roasting pan. Roast the bones, turning them occasionally, for about 1½ hours, or until they are richly browned. Remove the bones to a large soup pot.

2 Pour off and discard the fat from the roasting pan. Stir the boiling water into the pan, making sure to pick up the crusty, brown bits that stick to the bottom. To the bones in the soup pot, add the meat from the beef shank, cabbage, leeks, carrots, turnips, rutabaga, garlic, parsley, and dill. Stir in the beef broth and enough cold water so that the liquid generously covers the vegetables. Season with the salt and pepper.

▣ Set the soup pot over high heat. As the mixture comes to a boil, with a large spoon skim off any froth that rises to the top. Reduce the heat, cover, and simmer gently for 2½ hours. Uncover and continue to simmer for 30 minutes until the soup has reduced slightly and is richly flavored, adding more salt and pepper, if needed. Remove from the heat and set aside to cool slightly. Pull out the bones and the meat. With your finger, poke the marrow out of the bones, and stir into the soup. Discard the bones. Cut the shin meat into small pieces and return to the soup. Reheat and serve immediately, or cover and refrigerate overnight or for a couple of days and reheat to simmering before serving.

BIG APPLE BITE: The Dutch bought Manhattan from its Native American inhabitants for about twenty-four dollars worth of trinkets. Today, twenty-four dollars will buy you a cab ride from the Upper East Side to Queens.

HOMEMADE CHICKEN OR BEEF BROTH

Nothing beats real broth, which is why it's an excellent idea to keep a stash of it in your freezer. Frozen in 1-cup containers, the broth can be ready to use almost instantly after defrosting in the microwave or over low heat in a small, heavy saucepan.

Note that beef broth needs to be richer and darker than chicken broth, so the beef bones must be browned beforehand. Preheat the oven to 450ºF. Spread the bones in a lightly greased, shallow baking pan. Roast for 30 to 45 minutes, turning occasionally, until nicely browned. Proceed with the recipe below, using roasted beef bones in place of raw bones.

Makes about 12 cups

4 pounds chicken backs, necks, and wings, chopped into 2-inch pieces, or 4 pounds beef bones (see headnote), with just a little meat left on them	1 or 2 carrots, coarsely chopped
	5 sprigs fresh parsley
	1 tablespoon salt
2 large yellow onions, coarsely chopped	½ teaspoon crumbled dried thyme
1 large yellow onion, unpeeled and cut into large chunks	2 whole cloves
	8 black peppercorns
2 or 3 celery ribs, coarsely chopped	4 bay leaves

In a large pot, combine the chicken (or beef), chopped onions, the unpeeled onion, celery, carrots, parsley, salt, thyme, cloves, peppercorns, and bay leaves. Cover with 4 quarts of cold water. Bring to a boil over high heat, skimming off the foam as it rises to the surface with a large spoon. Lower the heat, and simmer very slowly and partly covered for about 3 hours. Set aside for an hour or so until slightly cooled.

Line a colander with a double thickness of damp cheesecloth, and set the colander over a large bowl. Pour the broth through the colander, discarding the solids. Cover the bowl, and refrigerate for several hours. As the broth chills, the fat will rise to the surface and solidify. Remove most of the fat, and discard it. (Keep in mind that some fat is necessary for flavor.) Pour the broth into 1-, 2-, or 4-cup containers with tight-fitting lids. The broth can be refrigerated for a few days or frozen for up to 6 months. If freezing, allow about ½ inch of headroom in each container.

IMPROVING CANNED BROTH

If there isn't time to make homemade broth, this may be the next best thing.

4 cans (13¼- or 14½-ounce) ready-to-serve canned clear chicken or beef broth	1 or 2 carrots, coarsely chopped
	3 sprigs fresh parsley
2 cups water	½ teaspoon crumbled dried thyme
1 large yellow onion, unpeeled and coarsely chopped	6 black peppercorns
6 celery ribs (including the leaves), coarsely chopped	1 bay leaf

In a large pot, combine the canned broth, water, onion, celery, carrots, parsley, thyme, peppercorns, and bay leaf, and bring to a boil over high heat. Reduce the heat, and simmer, partly covered, for about 30 minutes.

Line a colander with a double thickness of damp cheesecloth, and set the colander over a large bowl. Pour the broth through the colander, discarding the solids. Cool the broth and store as directed for homemade broth (previous recipe).

Cabbie: **Ismail Akbal**

Country of Origin: Turkey

Other Recipes:

Ladies' Navels (see page 180)

PROFILE: Five years ago this cabbie came to New York City to visit his uncle and liked it so much that he stayed. "I had no intention of coming to the United States on a permanent basis, but I couldn't believe all the opportunities there were here for an ambitious man," Ismail says. "Things have worked out very well for me. I married an American, who was an actress, and we have one child.

"I have always loved to cook. At one time I was chef-owner of a restaurant here in New York, and it was doing very well, but when my rent was doubled, I decided to close. I have no doubt that one day I will open another restaurant, but that's an expensive venture, and it may be a while before I can do it."

"Sebze Gorbas"

Turkish Vegetable Soup

"I think Americans believe that they are the only people in the world who depend on fast food some of the time," says Ismail. "That is not true, because this rich-tasting soup, which is similar to one my mother used to make, can be made from start to sit-down-and-eat in about an hour. If you like, you can make it early in the day or the day before and then reheat it when it will taste even better. With this I would serve a good bread, or even pita bread. A nice, fresh salad would taste good with it, too. Afterward, what else but Turkish coffee and a nice Turkish pastry?" (See Ismail's recipe for Ladies' Navels on page 180.)

MAKES ABOUT 8 CUPS;

4 TO 6 SERVINGS

1 tablespoon butter

1 tablespoon vegetable oil

½ to ¾ pound beef chuck, cut into small pieces
   (see Note, page 98)

1 medium-size zucchini, coarsely chopped (about
   1 heaping cup)

1 baking or boiling potato, coarsely chopped
   (about 1 cup)

2 slender carrots, thinly sliced (about 1 cup)

2 celery ribs, chopped (about 1 cup)

1 large yellow onion, chopped (about 1 cup)

2 cloves garlic, minced

1 teaspoon crumbled dried oregano

1 teaspoon salt

Freshly ground black pepper, to taste

½ pound plum tomatoes, seeded and chopped
   (see Note, page 122)

2 cups hot beef broth (see page 92), mixed with
   2 cups hot water

¼ cup coarsely chopped fresh parsley

1 Heat the butter and oil together in a Dutch oven or other large, heavy stew pot over high heat. When it is hot, add the beef, and cook, stirring and turning, until the meat has lost most of its red color. With a slotted spoon, remove the meat to a bowl and set aside.

2 To the fat and juices remaining in the pan, add the zucchini, potato, carrot, celery, onion, and garlic. Cook over medium-high heat, stirring almost constantly, until the vegetables have begun to cook down and soften, about 10 minutes. Stir in the oregano, salt, and pepper. Stir in the tomatoes until well blended. Return the beef to the pan, along with any juices that have accumulated in the bowl. Stir in the hot beef broth and water. Bring to a boil over high heat. Reduce the heat, cover, and simmer for 30 minutes. Stir in the parsley, and serve in warm soup bowls.

Cabbie: **Eman Abyseif**
Country of Origin: Egypt

Other Recipes:
Stuffed Grape Leaves (see page 20)

Lentil Soup

"Egyptians like meat in their diets," says Eman. "To eat with this vegetarian soup you can make a nice chicken salad with tomatoes and lettuce, or a beef salad would be good, too. My wife and I always eat warm pita bread or a flat bread (see *Chapati*, page 171), with soup." In this country, lentils—although grudgingly appreciated for their nutritional value—are generally considered dull and are consequently greatly underappreciated and underused. The fact is, though, that like potatoes and other starchy vegetables, as well as dried peas and beans, they have a unique ability to lap up the flavors of the ingredients with which they are combined, and this makes them a versatile base for soups, stews, and salads. Whenever you're cooking or dressing lentils, think of onions, garlic, sausage, herbs, spices, and other highly flavored ingredients. Lentils come in several colors besides brown, including yellow, green, red, and pink. All require slightly different cooking times, so consult package directions.

MAKES 4 TO 6 SERVINGS

1 cup brown lentils, rinsed and sorted as the package directs

2 tablespoons vegetable or olive oil

1 large yellow onion, chopped (about 1 cup)

2 cloves garlic, minced

1 serrano chile, seeded and minced (optional)

2 (14½-ounce) cans undrained diced tomatoes

2 cups water

1 teaspoon salt

¼ teaspoon freshly ground black pepper

▮ Place the lentils in a large, heavy saucepan, and add enough cold water to cover. Set aside for 30 minutes. Drain in a colander, and return the lentils to the saucepan. Add 3 cups of water. Place the pan over high heat, and bring to a boil. Reduce the heat to medium-low, and simmer until the lentils are tender and most of the water has been absorbed or cooked away, about 20 minutes. Transfer the lentils and any remaining liquid to a bowl and set aside.

▮ Add the oil to the same pan over medium-high heat. When the oil is hot, add the onion, and cook, stirring frequently, until softened, about 3 minutes. Stir in the garlic and chile, if using, and continue to cook, stirring occasionally, until the onion is golden, 3 to 5 minutes more. Stir in the lentils and any liquid in the bowl, the tomatoes and their canning liquid, the water, salt, and pepper, and bring to a simmer. Partially cover, and cook for about 20 minutes, stirring occasionally. Serve in warm, shallow soup bowls.

Cabbie: **Steve Kosefas**
Country of Origin: Greece

Other Recipes:
Arnaki Fornou: Greek-style Roast Leg of Lamb (see page 48)
Tomatoes Stuffed with Chopped Lamb and Rice (see page 120)

"Avgolemono"
Greek Egg and Lemon Soup with Chicken

Steve says that this is an authentic version of the very famous Greek chicken soup that is thickened mainly with egg yolks and cornstarch and spiked with fresh lemon juice. His family makes a whole meal of this hearty soup by serving it with a loaf of good, crusty Greek bread and a platter of cubed feta cheese sprinkled with dried oregano and lots of good kalamata olives. "In Greek homes, there is always a bottle of extra-virgin olive oil on the table, as well as a plate of lemon wedges," he adds.

MAKES 6 TO 8 SERVINGS

---

10 cups chicken broth (see page 92)
¾ cup raw converted white rice
2 tablespoons cornstarch
¼ to ⅓ cup freshly squeezed lemon juice
3 large egg yolks
2 to 3 cups finely cut cooked chicken
Salt and ground white pepper, to taste

▮ In a soup pot, bring the broth to a boil. Stir in the rice. Cover, and boil slowly until the rice is cooked, about 20 minutes.

▮ In a small bowl, stir the cornstarch into ¼ cup of the lemon juice until smooth, then stir into the boiling broth. Reduce the heat, and simmer the broth for 5 minutes.

3 In a small bowl, lightly beat the egg yolks. Stir a big spoonful of the hot broth into the yolks to temper them, then rapidly whisk the yolk mixture into the broth. Stir in the cooked chicken. When the broth returns to a simmer, adjust the seasoning, adding salt and additional lemon juice, if necessary. Season to taste with pepper. To serve, ladle the soup into warm, shallow soup bowls. Refrigerate the leftovers, and reheat gently.

Cabbie: **Julia Ortiz**
Country of Origin: Puerto Rico

Puerto Rican Chicken Soup

"If you are an American, this may not taste like the chicken soup your mama made," laughs Julia. "It has definite Latin American touches, like tomatoes, bell pepper, garlic, and cilantro. Cilantro, you know, has a very distinctive flavor that some people love, but others aren't crazy for, so parsley can be substituted. With bread, this can be a whole, delicious meal."

MAKES 6 SERVINGS

1 (3½- to 4-pound) boiler-fryer chicken, cut into 8 parts, and each breast cut crosswise into 2 pieces
8 cups cold water
2 teaspoons salt
1 medium-size yellow onion, chopped (about ½ cup)
1 carrot, peeled and chopped (about ¾ cup)
1 small red bell pepper, cored, seeded, and chopped (about 1 cup)
2 celery ribs, thinly sliced (about 1 cup)
2 medium-size tomatoes, seeded and chopped (about ¾ cup)
3 cloves garlic, minced
1 tablespoon chopped cilantro
3 tablespoons tomato paste, mixed with ½ cup water
1 tablespoon white vinegar
½ teaspoon freshly ground black pepper
1 cup raw converted white rice
Chopped cilantro, for garnish

1 Place the chicken in a soup pot, and add the cold water and salt. Bring to a boil over high heat, skimming off any foam that rises to the top with a large spoon. Reduce the heat, and simmer, covered, for 15 minutes. Stir in the onion, carrot, bell pepper, celery, tomato, garlic, cilantro, tomato-paste-and-water mixture, vinegar, pepper, and rice. Cover, and continue to simmer until the chicken is very tender, about 45 minutes.

3 To serve, ladle the soup into large, warm soup bowls, dividing the broth, vegetables, and chicken pieces evenly. Sprinkle each serving with chopped cilantro.

Cabbie: **Jacob Ginsberg**
Country of Origin: Russia

Beef Borscht

The common ingredient in all borscht recipes is beets. Some borschts are made with vegetables only, but others, like this one, contain meat, which makes it a much sturdier dish. A big spoonful of sour cream on top of each serving is a Russian tradition, as is the accompaniment of thick slices of black bread. "My wife always grates a little cucumber into the sour cream, which is not particularly Russian," Jacob says, "but I like it very much and I think you should do it this way."

MAKES 6 SERVINGS

2 pounds beef chuck, cut into 1½-inch cubes
(see Note)
2 cups beef broth (see page 92)
2 cups cold water
1 teaspoon salt
2 tablespoons butter
1 tablespoon vegetable oil
1 medium-size onion, chopped (about ½ cup)
2 cloves garlic, minced
3 medium-size beets, shredded (about 2 cups)
1 or 2 carrots, shredded (about 1 cup)
1 tablespoon sugar
¼ cup red wine vinegar
2 heaping cups shredded cabbage
1 (14½-ounce) can undrained diced tomatoes
Freshly ground black pepper, to taste
Sour cream, for serving

1 Place the beef cubes in a large pot, and cover with the beef broth and water. Add the salt and bring to a boil, skimming off the foam with a large spoon as it rises to the surface. Reduce the heat, then cover, and simmer slowly until the beef is very tender, about 1½ hours.

2 After the meat has cooked about 1 hour, in a large saucepan, heat together the butter and oil over high heat. When it is hot, stir in the onion and garlic, and cook over medium-high heat until the onion begins to soften, about 3 minutes. Stir in the beets and carrots until well blended. Sprinkle with the sugar, and stir in the vinegar. Cover, and cook over low heat, stirring occasionally, for 15 minutes. Stir in the cabbage until blended. Cover, and cook, stirring occasionally, for about 10 minutes longer. (If the mixture seems dry, stir in a spoonful or two of the beef cooking liquid.) Stir in the undrained tomatoes, then cover, and cook 10 minutes longer. Add the vegetable mixture to the meat mixture, and bring to a simmer. Cook, uncovered, for 15 minutes, or until the vegetables are very tender and the stew has thickened. Season with additional salt, if necessary, and plenty of freshly ground pepper.

To serve, ladle into warm, shallow soup bowls. Serve with sour cream.

The Best Stew Meat—Although the temptation to purchase lean stew meat, already cut into neat cubes, is mighty, you'll like the finished stew much better if you choose to buy a richly flavorful beef chuck roast or steak and cut the meat into cubes yourself. A chuck-eye roast is the best choice for stew meat, but any cut of chuck will work well.

Cabbie: **Nevio Frankovic**

Country of Origin: Yugoslavia

Other Recipes:

Spinach Salad (see page 159)

"Goulash"

Yugoslavian Meat Stew

"You can eat *goulash* with noodles or rice, but most people in Yugoslavia eat mashed potatoes with it," Nevio informs us. "Sometimes I mix the mashed potatoes with some cooked, chopped spinach or Swiss chard. That's good, too."

We used the meat from a 2⅓-pound sirloin half of a semiboneless leg of lamb. Because there is only one bone, it's easy enough to cut it out and then trim the meat of all exterior fat before cutting it into cubes.

MAKES 4 TO 6 SERVINGS

2 tablespoons vegetable oil

1½ to 1¾ pounds boneless lamb (preferably from the leg), trimmed of excess fat and cut into 1½-inch cubes

2 tablespoons butter

2 carrots, chopped (about 1½ cups)

1 large yellow onion, chopped (about 1 cup)

1 small green bell pepper, cored, seeded, and chopped (about 1 cup)

3 cloves garlic, minced

1 (14½-ounce) can undrained diced tomatoes

1 teaspoon salt

¼ teaspoon freshly ground black pepper

1 Heat the oil in a Dutch oven or other large, heavy stew pot over high heat. When it is hot, add the lamb, and cook, turning the meat and adjusting the heat as necessary, until crisp-brown on all sides. (This may take some time; be patient.) With a slotted spoon, remove the meat to a bowl and set aside. Pour off the grease in the pan, but leave all the brown, crusty bits in the bottom.

2 In the same pan, heat the butter over medium heat. When it bubbles, stir in the carrots, onion, and bell pepper. Cook, stir-

ring almost constantly, until the vegetables are soft and starting to brown, about 10 minutes. Stir in the garlic until softened, about 1 minute longer. Stir in the undrained tomatoes, salt, and pepper, and bring the mixture to a simmer. Remove from the heat and set aside to cool slightly, about 15 minutes, stirring occasionally.

■ Spoon the cooled vegetable mixture into a food processor or blender. (Do not rinse the cooking pan, as you will continue to use it.) Process the vegetables until smooth. (If using a blender, this will have to be done in two batches and a little water may have to be added. You may also do this in the cooking pan if using an immersion blender.) Return the meat to the cooking pan, including the juices that have collected in the bowl. Stir in the puréed vegetables. Bring to a simmer over high heat, stirring frequently. Reduce the heat, cover, and simmer gently for 15 minutes, stirring a few times. Uncover the pan, and continue to simmer, stirring frequently, especially toward the end of the cooking time, until the meat is tender, about 15 minutes.

Cabbie: **Bill Forst**

Country of Origin: Austria and Denmark

Beef Flanken and Vegetable Stew

"This soup has a lot of flavor," says Bill, who has been driving a cab off and on for more than forty years, "which is why I always eat it with plenty of mustard, although some people like horseradish. One thing is for sure: you must drink beer with this—any kind of beer. "

This recipe calls for flanken, a special cut that comes from the chuck (shoulder portion) of the beef. It is a thin strip of meat containing portions of the first five cross-cut ribs. Flanken is extremely flavorful, but needs long, slow cooking, which makes it exquisite stew meat.

MAKES 6 SERVINGS

------

2 pounds beef flanken (see headnote)

Salt and freshly ground black pepper, to taste

⅓ cup all-purpose flour

2 to 3 tablespoons vegetable oil

2 medium-size yellow onions, sliced (about 2 cups)

1 cup beef broth (see page 92)

1½ cups cold water

4 carrots, trimmed, lightly scraped, and cut into ½-inch slices (about 2 cups)

4 celery ribs, cut into ½-inch slices (about 2 cups)

4 medium-size boiling potatoes (about 1 pound), cut into bite-size pieces

½ pound green beans, trimmed and cut into 1-inch lengths

Dark German mustard, for serving

Prepared horseradish, for serving

1 Season the flanken with salt and pepper. Sprinkle the flour on a sheet of waxed paper. Dredge the flanken in the flour until well coated. Reserve about 2 tablespoons of the remaining flour.

2 Heat the oil in a Dutch oven or other large, heavy stew pot over medium-high heat. When it is hot, add the flanken, and cook, turning the meat and adjusting the heat as necessary, until each piece is nicely browned. With tongs, remove the meat from the pan and set aside. Add the onion to the drippings in the pan (another tablespoon of oil can be added, if needed), and cook, stirring occasionally, until lightly browned, about 8 minutes. With a slotted spoon, remove the onion to a bowl and set aside.

3 Pour off and discard any drippings remaining in the pan, leaving just the crusty, brown bits that cling to the bottom. Stir together the beef broth and water in the pan. Return the meat and onions to the pan. Bring to a slow boil over high heat. Reduce the heat, cover, and simmer gently for 1 hour. Add the carrots, celery, and potatoes, and continue to cook for 30 minutes. Stir in the green beans, and continue to cook for another 30 minutes, or until the meat is very tender and the potatoes and carrots are ready to fall apart.

4 In a small bowl, gradually whisk about 1 cup of the hot stew liquid with the 2 tablespoons of reserved flour until smooth. Stir the flour mixture into the stew, and cook, stirring, until bubbling and slightly thickened. Season with salt and pepper. Serve with mustard and prepared horseradish.

BIG APPLE BITE: Babe Ruth hit his first home run in Yankee Stadium in the first game ever played there.

Cabbie: **Adama Tall**

Country of Origin: Republic of Senegal

Senegalese Beef Stew with Egg and Vegetable Salad

"Serving stew surrounded by salad from a big platter is very much a Senegalese custom," says Adama. "It looks very pretty and my American friends are all very impressed when I do it this way. Therefore, I am pleased to give you my best recipes. There is a strong French influence in Senegal, which makes me prefer French bread with my meals. The French bread in New York is very good, and I know the best places to buy it." Adama and his family drink ginger beer or fruit juice with their meals. "Alcohol is taboo for the Senegalese," he explains.

What makes this stew unique is that it cooks so quickly, a big departure from more traditional stews that require long, slow cooking. The meat—a tender sirloin steak—is cooked only to medium-rare, and the presentation of the stew at the center of a colorful salad is a striking and decidedly French touch.

MAKES 4 TO 6 SERVINGS

2 tablespoons vegetable oil

1½ pounds sirloin or other tender steak, 1 inch thick, cut into 1-inch cubes

1 medium-size yellow onion, finely chopped (about ½ cup)

2 cloves garlic, minced

1 tablespoon Dijon mustard

⅓ cup water

1 tablespoon red wine vinegar

Salt and freshly ground black pepper, to taste

Chopped fresh parsley, for garnish

Egg and Vegetable Salad (recipe follows), for serving

1 Heat the oil in a large skillet over high heat. When it is very hot, add the steak cubes, and cook, turning, until they are nicely browned and done to the rare or medium-rare stage, adjusting the heat as necessary. This should take no longer than 4 to 5 minutes. With a slotted spoon, remove the steak cubes to a plate and set aside.

2 Add the onion and garlic to the drippings in the skillet, and cook over medium heat, stirring, just until the onion and garlic are softened, about 3 minutes. Stir in the mustard until well blended. Stir in the water and vinegar. Cook over medium-high heat, stirring almost constantly, until the sauce has thickened to a gravy-like consistency, 6 to 8 minutes. Return the meat and any juice that has accumulated on the plate to the skillet. Cook, stirring, just until the meat is heated through. Season to taste with salt and pepper.

3 Spoon the stew in the center of a large platter, leaving room for the salad around

the edges. Sprinkle with the parsley. Spoon the Egg and Vegetable Salad around the stew, and serve immediately.

Egg and Vegetable Salad

MAKES 4 TO 6 SERVINGS

2 small boiling potatoes, peeled and cut into ¼-inch slices (about 1½ cups)

⅓ cup vegetable oil

⅓ cup red wine vinegar

½ teaspoon chicken bouillon granules or powder, dissolved in 1 tablespoon boiling water

Salt and freshly ground black pepper, to taste

1 romaine lettuce heart (the pale green leaf core), cut crosswise into narrow strips (about 6 cups)

1 small red onion, thinly sliced and the slices separated into rings (about ½ cup)

About 18 cherry tomatoes, cut in half

4 hard-cooked eggs, peeled and chilled

1. In a medium-size saucepan, cook the potato slices in lightly salted boiling water until just tender, 4 to 5 minutes. Drain into a colander, and transfer to a large bowl.

2. To make the dressing, in a medium-size bowl, whisk together the oil, vinegar, and dissolved bouillon. Season with salt and pepper. Add about half of the dressing to the warm potatoes, tossing until they are well coated, and set aside.

3. Just before serving, add the lettuce, onion rings, and tomatoes to the potato slices, and toss with the remaining dressing. Cut each egg crosswise into about 4 slices. Spoon the salad around the stew, and garnish with the egg slices.

BIG APPLE BITE: Don't be surprised if you hear a lot of people speaking Spanish in New York. There are more Puerto Ricans living in the New York metropolitan area than there are in Puerto Rico itself.

Cabbie: **Mamady Kaba**

Country of Origin: Guinea

Beef Stew
with Peanut Sauce

"Ever since there has been an Africa, I think there has been some form of peanut sauce," says Mamady. "It adds a richness that I cannot explain, but I urge you to try it, although this stew would be good without it. We serve our stew over a nice, fluffy, white rice and have a salad, too. We also have French bread on the table, even though there is rice. My family likes fruit for dessert, so there is a bowl of cut-up fruits. We favor pineapple, bananas, and oranges, especially. I have also discovered that I like apples, something we don't have in my country, so sometimes I add them to the bowl. We drink fruit juice with the meal and serve strong French coffee afterward."

MAKES 4 TO 6 SERVINGS

1½ pounds beef chuck (see Note, page 98)

1 small onion, shredded (about ¼ cup)

1 teaspoon salt

½ teaspoon freshly ground black pepper

2 tablespoons vegetable oil

4 cloves garlic, minced

1 medium-size tomato, seeded and chopped
  (see Note, page 122)

3 tablespoons tomato paste, mixed into 2 cups water

¼ cup creamy peanut butter (do not use
  natural-style)

White rice, cooked as directed on package

1 Trim away any excess fat from the edges of the meat. Cut the meat into 1-inch cubes. In a medium-size bowl, mix together the onion, salt, and pepper. Add the beef cubes and turn them with your hands until they are completely coated with the onion mixture. Cover and refrigerate for at least 1 hour or up to several hours.

2 Heat the oil in a large skillet over high heat. When it is very hot, add the beef cubes, including any of the onion mixture that remains in the bowl. Cook, stirring and turning, until the meat has lost its raw look. Stir in the garlic, and cook briefly, just until slightly softened, about 1 minute. Stir in the tomato. Add the tomato paste-and-water mixture. Bring to a boil, then reduce the heat until the mixture simmers. Stir in the peanut butter until well blended. Continue to simmer, covered, until the meat is fork-tender, about 45 minutes. After about 30 minutes, if the stew seems too thin, increase the heat slightly and cook, uncovered, stirring occasionally for the last 10 or 15 minutes. Serve over hot cooked rice.

Cabbie: **Luis Artchabala**

Country of Origin: Ecuador

Other Recipes:

Fried Yuca with Pickled Onion Rings (see page 155)

Cassata: Sicilian Special-occasion Pound Cake (see page 186)

PROFILE: "I have been in this country for about twenty years and driving a cab for nearly half that time," says Luis. "Because I live alone, I have to cook for myself, but that's okay, because back at home I always watched my mother and grandmother cook, and I learned a lot about our ways of preparing food."

"Seco de Pollo"

Saffron-flavored Chicken and Vegetables

"This is a recipe I think Americans will enjoy," says Luis. "When I was a boy, I raised my family's chickens, and this is one of the ways my mother cooked chicken for us. The only difference between this recipe and hers is that she always chopped some hot chile peppers—like serranos or jalapeños—for us to stir in at the table. Pilsner beer is very refreshing to drink with this, but so is sparkling water. If I'm having company, I serve *Cassata* (see page 186) for dessert, which is definitely not from Ecuador."

MAKES 4 TO 6 SERVINGS

1 (3½- to 4-pound) broiler-fryer chicken, cut into 8 parts

Salt and freshly ground black pepper, to taste

2 tablespoons lard, or solid white vegetable shortening

1 medium-size yellow onion, chopped (about ½ cup)

2 cloves garlic, minced

1 small green bell pepper, cored, seeded, and chopped (about 1 cup)

1 large tomato, seeded and chopped (See Note, page 122)

Big pinch of saffron threads (see Note)

1 large boiling potato, peeled and cut into small pieces (about 1 cup)

1 Season the chicken pieces with salt and pepper. Heat the lard in a Dutch oven or other large, heavy stew pot over high heat. When the lard is hot, add the chicken pieces, skin-side down, and lightly brown on all sides, adjusting the heat as necessary. Remove the chicken to a plate and set aside.

2 Discard all but about 1 tablespoon of the fat left in the pan. Stir in the onion, garlic, and bell pepper, and cook over medium-high heat, stirring, just until softened, about 3 minutes. Stir in the tomato.

Return the chicken, skin-side up, to the pan and add enough cold water to barely come up and around the chicken (1½ to 2 cups, more or less, depending on the size of the pan). Bring to a boil, then lower the heat and simmer, uncovered, for 20 minutes.

▧ Meanwhile, place the saffron in a small bowl and add about 1 tablespoon of the cooking liquid. After the chicken has cooked for 20 minutes, stir the potato and the saffron-infused liquid into the chicken mixture. Continue to cook, uncovered, until the potato pieces are very soft and the sauce has thickened slightly, about 30

minutes. Mash some of the potato pieces with the back of a fork, then season the stew to taste with salt and pepper before serving over rice.

NOTE: Saffron, which resembles tiny, bright orange threads, is the stigma from a small purple crocus. Since each stigma is handpicked and then carefully dried, it's no wonder saffron is the world's most expensive spice and, ounce for ounce, one of the most valuable things in the world. Fortunately, a little saffron goes a long way. But to get the most flavor per pinch, soak the saffron threads in a small amount of hot cooking liquid, or even water, for 15 or 20 minutes. When ready to use, add both the saffron and the soaking liquid to the dish you are cooking.

BIG APPLE BITE: New York City was briefly the U.S. capital from 1789 to 1790. Before moving to 1600 Pennsylvania Avenue, the presidential residence was located on Cherry Street in a mansion called "The Palace." The residence has since been demolished, and the location serves as a granite support for the Brooklyn Bridge.

Cabbies: **Anna and Peter Egan**
Country of Origin: Ireland and the United States

Other Recipes:

Glazed Corned Beef with Vegetables (see page 41)
Mashed Potatoes, Carrots, and Parsnips (see page 147)
Irish Soda Bread (see page 170)
Emerald Isle Trifle (see page 189)

Irish Lamb Stew

"In Ireland, the season for damp, cold days is a long one," says Anna, "which probably accounts for why we eat so many good, rib-sticking stews. Here is a recipe my mother used to make for us. It is real Irish comfort food, and may even be better a day or two after it's made." (In that case, make sure to reheat it just to the simmering point or the lamb meat will get stringy.) Bread, of course, is the natural accompaniment. "A plain homemade loaf is very good," Anna says, "but fresh-baked Irish Soda Bread (see page 170) is sublime!"

MAKES 6 SERVINGS

1½ pounds lamb neck, cut into chunks
2 large yellow onions, chopped
  (about 2 cups)
2 carrots, peeled and chopped (about 1 cup)
2 small turnips, chopped (about 1 cup)
1 or 2 parsnips, chopped (about 1 cup)
1 tablespoon salt
¾ cup pearl barley
Freshly ground black pepper, to taste

1 Place the lamb, onions, carrots, turnips, parsnips, and salt in a large soup pot. Add enough cold water to cover. Bring the mixture to a boil over high heat. Reduce the heat, cover, and simmer until the meat is tender, 1½ to 2 hours. Remove from the heat, and set aside to cool slightly. Skim off any fat that rises to the surface, and discard. With a slotted spoon, remove the meat to a plate and set aside.

2 Stir the barley into the pot, and return to medium-high heat. Cover, and continue to simmer until the barley is tender, about 30 minutes. Season with pepper. Meanwhile, pull the meat from the neck bones and cut it into small pieces. Return the meat to the stew, stirring just until the meat is heated through. If the stew seems a little thick, particularly if you are heating leftovers, thin it with water.

Cabbie: **Hakim Anes**

Country of Origin: Algeria

Other Recipes:

Sesame-Orange Sliced Cookies (see page 192)

PROFILE: Before coming to the United States seven years ago, thirty-one-year-old Hakim was studying industrial mechanical engineering in Algiers. In New York, driving a cab allows him the time to pursue his dream of becoming an actor.

Algerian-style Couscous with Lamb and Little Glazed Onions

"My mother is a perfect cook," says Hakim. "When I came to America she gave me many of her recipes. Only some I have learned to make and it is a struggle, because men don't cook in my country. This is a recipe that is often served on holidays and special occasions. At these times, we definitely use the toasted almonds and glazed onions, but not always for a regular meal. For dessert, my mother always served fresh fruit—grapes, fresh dates, and wedges of cantaloupe or honeydew—whatever is ripe and good. And later there was always something sweet, like Sesame-Orange Sliced Cookies (see page 192), along with strong French coffee served in tiny cups. It is the custom in my country for the whole family to eat together. Not like here where everybody is in a rush and eats separately."

MAKES 6 TO 8 SERVINGS

3 tablespoons butter

1 medium-size yellow onion, chopped (about ½ cup)

3 cloves garlic, minced

2 teaspoons salt

1 teaspoon freshly ground black pepper

½ teaspoon ground ginger

Pinch saffron threads, crumbled

2 pounds boneless leg of lamb, trimmed of most of the fat and cut into 1½-inch chunks

4 medium-size turnips (about 1 pound), peeled and cut into quarters

4 small zucchini (about 1 pound), cut into 1-inch pieces

2 cups peeled baby carrots

2 (15½-ounce) cans chickpeas, drained and rinsed

1 (10-ounce) box plain couscous

2 tablespoons lightly browned melted butter

½ cup slivered almonds, toasted (see Note, page 175), for garnish

Little Glazed Onions (recipe follows), for serving

■ In a Dutch oven or other large, heavy stew pot, melt the 3 tablespoons butter over medium-low heat. Stir in the onion, garlic, salt, pepper, ginger, and saffron, and cook just until the mixture is hot. Add the lamb, and cook, turning with a large spoon, until the meat chunks are evenly coated with the butter mixture and have lost their raw color. Add enough water to cover the lamb, and bring to a simmer. With a large spoon, skim off any foam that rises to the surface. Cover tightly and simmer gently until the meat is tender, about 1 hour. Increase the heat, and add the turnips, zucchini, carrots, and chickpeas. When the mixture comes to a boil, reduce the heat, cover, and simmer until the vegetables are tender, about 20 minutes.

2 Meanwhile, prepare the couscous according to the package directions, substituting cooking broth for the water and eliminating the salt and the oil. When the couscous has finished steaming, stir in the 2 tablespoons browned butter, and toss until well blended.

3 To serve, spoon the couscous into the center of a large platter. With a slotted spoon, remove the meat and vegetables from the pot, and spoon around the couscous. Scatter the almonds over the couscous, and serve with Little Glazed Onions. The broth remaining in the stew pot can be served in a sauceboat and used to moisten the couscous.

Little Glazed Onions

MAKES ABOUT 2 CUPS

1 (16-ounce) bag frozen small whole onions
½ cup reserved cooking broth from the lamb
2 tablespoons butter
2 tablespoons honey

Cook the onions according to the package directions, but reduce the cooking time by about half. Drain the onions and transfer them to a large skillet, along with the broth, butter, and honey. Bring to a boil, then reduce the heat to medium, and cook, stirring frequently, until the onions are glazed and golden, about 15 minutes. A little more broth may have to be added toward the end of the cooking time so that the onions glaze evenly and don't stick to the skillet.

BIG APPLE BITE: The Bronx Zoo is the largest metropolitan zoo in the United States—it's also home to more than 6,400 animals.

Cabbie: **Hamdy A. Osman**

Country of Origin: Egypt

"Kosheree"

Macaroni, Chickpea, and Rice Stew with Buttered Okra

"With this," says Hamdy, "my family also eats a warm pita bread, okra, and we drink a nice fruit juice or soda. We finish the meal with a beautiful rice pudding made with golden raisins and dusted with cinnamon."

Precede this platter with Middle Eastern Chopped Salad with Tahini Dressing (see page 162), and you have a spectacular vegetarian meal. We liked our *kosheree* served with tiny, broiled lamb rib chops, which is a good idea when the diners are meat lovers."

MAKES 4 TO 6 SERVINGS

3 tablespoons extra-virgin olive oil

1 large yellow onion, finely chopped
  (about 1 cup)

4 cloves garlic, minced

1 (15-ounce) can tomato sauce

1 tablespoon freshly squeezed lemon juice

½ teaspoon crushed red pepper

2 cups raw elbow macaroni (about
  4 cups cooked)

1½ cups raw converted white rice (about
  4½ cups cooked)

1 (19-ounce) can chickpeas (garbanzo beans),
  drained and rinsed

Sliced, kosher-style dill pickles, for serving

Buttered Okra (recipe follows), for serving

1 Heat 2 tablespoons of the oil in a large skillet over high heat. When it is hot, add the onion, and cook over medium-high heat, stirring frequently, until the onion is softened, 3 to 5 minutes. Stir in the garlic, and cook briefly just until the garlic is softened, about 1 minute longer. Stir in the tomato sauce, lemon juice, and red pepper. Bring the mixture to a slow simmer, and cook, stirring frequently, for 5 minutes. Remove from the heat and set aside.

2 Cook the macaroni and rice separately in salted water, following the package directions, timing things so that both are done at about the same time. In a small saucepan, heat the remaining tablespoon of oil with the chickpeas, and cook over medium heat, stirring gently, until the beans are hot. Reheat the tomato sauce.

3 To serve, arrange the warm macaroni, rice, and garbanzo beans on a platter in three separate mounds. Pour the hot tomato sauce over everything, and surround with the pickle slices. Serve with Buttered Okra on the side.

Buttered Okra

4 tablespoons (½ stick) butter
4 cloves garlic, thinly slivered
1 pound fresh okra
Salt and freshly ground black pepper, to taste

▮ Bring a large pot of salted water to a boil.

▮ Place the butter and garlic in a small heavy saucepan set over very low heat. Cook, stirring frequently, until the garlic is very soft, about 15 minutes, but do not allow either the butter or the garlic to brown. Remove from the heat, and set aside.

▮ Trim the stems from the okra and cut each pod into ¼-inch slices. Drop the okra into the pot of boiling, salted water. Cover, and simmer until the okra is barely tender, about 3 minutes. Drain into a colander, and return to the cooking pan. Add the garlic and butter, and toss until blended. Season with salt and pepper, and serve immediately.

BIG APPLE BITE: In 1985, two men carrying large "knapsacks" took the elevator to the observation deck of the Empire State Building. The knapsacks turned out to be parachutes, and the sneaky two gleefully jumped eighty-six stories down into the evening rush-hour traffic below. Wasting no time, they bundled up their chutes, hailed separate taxis, and sped off down Fifth Avenue, never to be seen or heard from again.

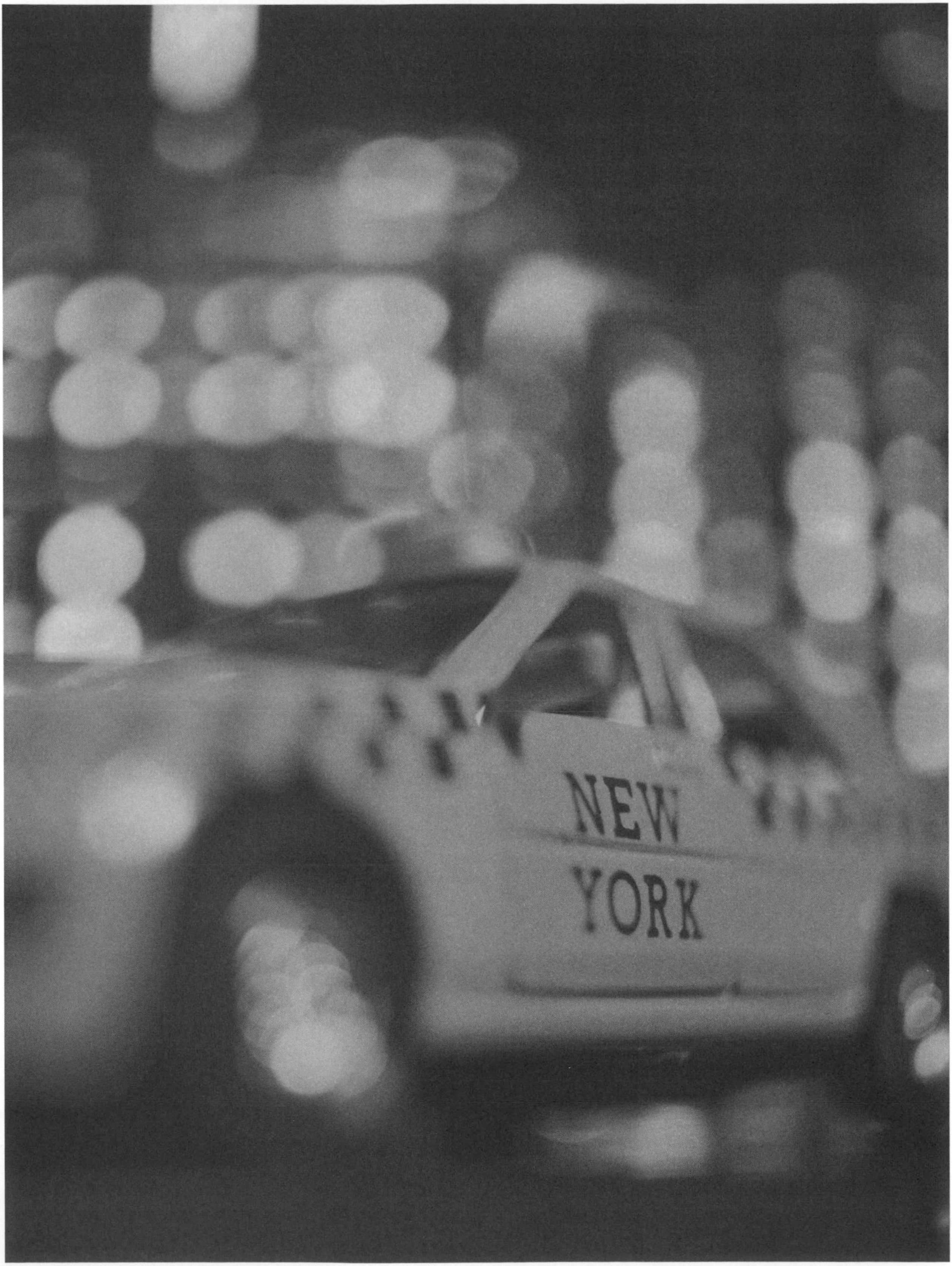
NEW
YORK

Chapter 5 Appetizers and First Courses Meat and Poultry Fish and Seafood Hearty Soups and Stews Casseroles and Skillet Meals Side Dishes and Salads Breads and Baked Goods Desserts and Other Sweet Things Appetizers and First Courses Meat and Poultry Fish and Seafood Hearty Soups and Stews Casseroles and Skillet Meals Side Dishes and Salads Breads and Baked Goods Desserts and Other Sweet Things Appetizers and First Courses Meat and Poultry Fish and Seafood Hearty Soups and Stews Casseroles and Skillet Meals Side Dishes and Salads Breads and Baked Goods Desserts Other Sweet Things Appetizers and First Courses Meat and Poultry Fish and Seafood Hearty Soups and Stews Casseroles and Skillet Meals Side Dishes and Salads Breads and Baked Goods Desserts Other Sweet Things Appetizers and First Courses Meat and Poultry Fish and Seafood Hearty Soups and Stews Casseroles and Skillet Meals Side Dishes and Salads Breads and Baked Goods Desserts and Other Sweet Things Appetizers and First Courses Meat and Poultry Fish and Seafood Hearty Soups and Stews Casseroles and Skillet Meals Side Dishes and Salads Breads and Baked Goods Desserts and Other Sweet Things Appetizers and First Courses Meat and Poultry Fish and Seafood Hearty Soups and Stews **Casseroles and Skillet Meals** Side Dishes and Salads Breads and Baked Goods Desserts and Other Sweet Things Appetizers and First Courses Meat and Poultry Fish Seafood Hearty Soups and Stews Casseroles and Skillet Meals Side Dishes and Salads Breads and Baked Goods Desserts and Other Sweet Things Appetizers and First Courses Meat and Poultry Fish and Seafood Hearty Soups and Stews Casseroles and Skillet Meals Side Dishes and Salads Breads Baked Goods Desserts and Other Sweet Things Appetizers and First Courses Meat and Poultry Fish and Seafood Hearty Soups and Stews Casseroles and Skillet Meals Side Dishes and Salads Breads and Baked Goods Desserts and Other Sweet Things Appetizers and First Courses Meat and Poultry Fish and Seafood Hearty Soups and Stews Casseroles and Skillet Meals Side Dishes and Salads Breads and Baked Goods Desserts and Other Sweet Things Appetizers and First Courses Meat and Poultry Fish and Seafood Hearty Soups and Stews Casseroles and Skillet Meals Side Dishes and Salads Breads and Baked Goods Desserts and Other Sweet Things Appetizers and First Courses Meat and Poultry Fish and Seafood Hearty Soups and Stews Casseroles and Skillet Meals Side Dishes and Salads Breads and Baked Goods Desserts and Other Sweet Things Appetizers and First Courses Meat and Poultry Fish and Seafood Hearty Soups and Stews Casseroles and Skillet Meals Side Dishes and Salads Breads and Baked Goods Desserts and Other Sweet Things Appetizers and First Courses Meat and Poultry Fish and Seafood Hearty Soups and Stews Casseroles Skillet Meals Side Dishes and Salads Breads and Baked Goods Desserts and Other Sweet Things

TAXI TRIVIA: According to the NYC Taxi & Limousine Commission, there are more than seven hundred minivan cabs in operation in New York City.

Cabbie: **Dennis Launer**

Country of Origin: United States

Other Recipes:

Pan-Broiled Mako Shark (or Swordfish) Steaks (see page 80)

Gingered New Potatoes (see page 146)

Steamed Bok Choy (see page 154)

Stuffed Cabbage in Sweet Tomato Sauce

"This recipe comes from my mother's friend, Doris," Dennis says. "And it is the best stuffed cabbage you have ever eaten. I guarantee it! With this I would serve a green salad and warm buttered rolls to sop up all of the wonderful sauce. One other thing you should know, these rolls are even better a day or two later, and they reheat very nicely in a microwave or even a double-boiler."

Savoy cabbage leaves (the dark green, crinkled variety) tend to come off the head more easily than those of the more common green cabbage. In order to make sure you end up with twelve large leaves, we discovered that it was easier to remove six leaves from each of two cabbages, and save the remainder of the heads for other uses.

A regular shallow skillet is too small to fit all of the cabbage rolls plus the sauce in one layer. For this recipe, you will need a large, deep skillet (at least 12 inches in diameter with a 2½- to 3-inch side) with a lid. You can improvise by using a small, heavy roasting pan and covering it tightly with heavy-duty aluminum foil.

MAKES 6 TO 12 SERVINGS

2 heads Savoy cabbage

1½ pounds ground beef (90 percent lean)

1 cup cooked brown rice (⅓ cup raw rice)

1 large egg, lightly beaten

1 teaspoon salt

¼ teaspoon freshly ground black pepper

1 tablespoon vegetable oil

1 small yellow onion, finely chopped (about ¼ cup)

1 (46-ounce) can or bottle tomato juice

2 tablespoons sugar

⅓ cup dark raisins

1 Pull off any wilted leaves from the cabbages, and cut out the cores. Carefully pull away 6 leaves from each head, reserving the remainder of the heads for other uses. Cut out the tough core section at the bottom of each leaf in the shape of a V. Set the leaves aside.

2 Fill a large pot with salted water. Bring to a boil over high heat. Boil the leaves, 2 or 3 at a time, until they are slightly limp, about 3 minutes. With tongs, grasp each leaf by the core end, remove it from the pot, and lay each one flat on layers of paper towels to drain.

▨ In a large bowl, with your hands, gently mix together the ground beef, cooked rice, egg, salt, and pepper until well blended. The mixture will be very moist. Have ready a ⅓-cup dry measuring cup.

▨ On a work surface, lay out one cabbage leaf, cupped-side up. Scoop out the ground beef mixture with the measuring cup and form it into an oval patty. Set the patty on the bottom third of the cabbage leaf. Roll the bottom up and over the filling, then fold in the sides and roll up. Set aside with the seam side down. Repeat with the remaining leaves and ground beef mixture, and set aside.

▨ Heat the oil in a large, deep skillet (at least 12 inches) over high heat. Stir in the onion, and cook over medium heat until tender, 3 to 5 minutes. Stir in the tomato juice, sugar, and raisins until well blended. Simmer over medium heat for about 15 minutes to give the flavors time to blend and for the sauce to cook down slightly. Arrange the rolls seam-side down in the sauce. Spoon the sauce over the tops of the rolls. Cover tightly and simmer very gently for 45 minutes. At this point, the cabbage leaves will be very tender and the filling will be cooked through. (This recipe can be prepared 1 hour or so ahead up to this point and very gently reheated. If you want to make it a day or so ahead, cool, cover, and refrigerate. Bring to room temperature before reheating.)

BIG APPLE BITE: Because of the efficient grid mapping system in New York, engineers managed to squeeze 6,374.6 miles of streets into the city.

Cabbie: **Sophie Polykratis**
Country of Origin: Greece

"Pastitsio"
Greek Macaroni Pie

"This is a dish that is closely associated with Greek cooking," Sophie tells us, "although it is usually reserved for the feasting period called 'Carnival' that precedes Lenten fasting. One interesting thing about béchamel sauce, which I learned from one of my chef teachers, is that béchamel is a Greek creation, and is not French as most people think. The oregano I call for is Greek oregano, which is more pungent than the Italian oregano most Americans are used to. You can find it in most ethnic grocery stores, but if not, just use a little more of the Italian."

Kefalotiri is a hard, Greek grating cheese. Many well-stocked supermarket cheese departments carry it, and most cheese stores keep it in stock, but a really good Parmesan cheese can be used as a substitute.

"I usually make a nice Greek Salad (see page 30) to go with this very rich pie, and pour a nice white wine from Crete."

MAKES 8 SERVINGS

Meat Sauce
2 tablespoons olive oil
1 large yellow onion, finely chopped
  (about 1 cup)
2 cloves garlic, minced
1 pound ground beef (90 percent lean)
1½ teaspoons dried oregano leaves (Greek,
  if possible), crumbled
½ teaspoon salt
⅛ teaspoon freshly ground black pepper
½ cup canned tomato sauce

2-inch cinnamon stick
5 whole cloves, tied into a small piece
  of cheesecloth

Pasta
8 ounces bucatini or perciatelli (a thin,
  hollow spaghetti), broken in half

Béchamel Sauce
½ cup all-purpose flour
¼ pound (1 stick) butter
6 cups whole milk

2 large eggs

1 teaspoon salt

⅛ teaspoon ground white pepper

Topping

1 cup freshly grated *Kefalotiri* or good-quality
  Parmesan cheese

1 cup zwieback crumbs (ground up in a food
  processor, see Note)

1 Prepare the Meat Sauce: Heat the oil in a large skillet set over medium-high heat. Add the onion, and cook, stirring frequently, until softened, 3 to 5 minutes. Stir in the garlic, and cook just until softened, about 1 minute more. Add the ground beef, and cook, breaking up the meat with the side of a spoon, until it is crumbled and no pink remains. Stir in the oregano, salt, and pepper until well blended. Stir in the tomato sauce, cinnamon stick, and cheesecloth packet of cloves. Reduce the heat, and simmer, covered, for 20 minutes. Uncover, and continue to cook, stirring, until most of the liquid has evaporated and been absorbed into the meat. Remove from the heat and set aside.

2 While the meat sauce is cooking, boil the pasta in a large pot of lightly salted water until barely tender, about 10 minutes. Drain into a colander and rinse very well with cold water, and set aside.

3 Preheat the oven to 350°F. Grease a 13 x 9-inch baking dish and set aside.

4 Prepare the Béchamel Sauce: Heat the butter in a large, heavy saucepan over medium heat until bubbly. Add the flour, and cook, stirring constantly, until the mixture bubbles. Rapidly whisk in the milk, and continue to cook, stirring with the whisk, until the sauce simmers and is thick and smooth. Remove from the heat.

5 In a small bowl, beat the eggs until well blended. Stir a couple of spoonsful of the hot milk mixture into the eggs to temper them, then rapidly whisk the egg mixture into the milk mixture. Season with salt and white pepper.

6 Evenly arrange half the pasta in the bottom of the prepared baking dish and sprinkle evenly with half the cheese. Remove the cinnamon stick and cloves from the meat sauce. Spoon all the meat sauce over the pasta. Add the remaining pasta, and sprinkle evenly with the remaining cheese. Spoon the béchamel sauce evenly over the top, smoothing it lightly with the back of a spoon. Sprinkle evenly with the crumbs.

7 Bake for about 30 minutes, or until hot and bubbly. Remove from the oven and let stand for about 20 minutes before cutting into serving portions.

NOTE: Zwieback most resembles *paximadi*, the very slightly sweetened, twice-baked Greek bread that is traditionally used for making the bread-crumb topping for this dish. *Paximadi* is available in all Greek and Middle Eastern grocery stores. Regular bread crumbs are not a good substitute.

Cabbie: **Anthony Kaloudaki**
Country of Origin: Greece

"Moussaka"

"My grandmother and mother have been cooking for our family since I can remember, and I have never tasted better food anywhere," says Anthony. "Now my daughter is learning." Anthoula, his wife, serves her *moussaka* with what she describes as "a beautiful salad" made with many tender little greens, sliced cucumber, and tomato wedges dressed with a simple mixture of fresh lemon juice and extra-virgin olive oil that has been seasoned with dried, crumbled oregano, salt, and freshly ground pepper. "A good bread," she adds, "which we dip into a fruity olive oil, is also essential."

The *graviera* cheese called for in this recipe is the Greek version of Swiss Gruyère, which can be used as a substitute. Hristos Soulantzos' Crusty Country Bread (see page 168) is the perfect bread for serving with any Greek meal.

MAKES 8 TO 10 SERVINGS

1 slender purple eggplant, weighing about 1½ pounds, trimmed, peeled, and sliced crosswise into ½-inch-thick slices

Salt

All-purpose flour, for dredging

Olive or vegetable oil

2½ pounds ground beef (85 percent lean) or lean ground lamb (preferably from the leg)

1 medium-size yellow onion, finely chopped (about ½ cup)

3 cloves garlic, minced

1 cup whole, peeled, canned tomatoes, drained and chopped

1 cup dry white wine or dry vermouth

2 tablespoons tomato paste

2 bay leaves

3-inch cinnamon stick

4 whole allspice, tied into a piece of cheesecloth

Freshly ground black pepper, to taste

½ cup grated **graviera** or Swiss Gruyère cheese

2 tablespoons chopped fresh parsley

¼ teaspoon ground nutmeg

Béchamel Sauce

6 tablespoons unsalted butter

6 tablespoons all-purpose flour

4 cups whole milk

1 teaspoon salt

½ teaspoon ground nutmeg

⅛ teaspoon ground white pepper

2 large eggs

1 Sprinkle the eggplant slices with salt and set them aside on several thicknesses of paper towels to drain for about 30 minutes, to draw out some of the bitterness.

2 Preheat the oven to 400°F. Grease and flour a 13 x 9-inch glass baking dish and set aside. Sprinkle the flour for dredging on a sheet of waxed paper. Lightly coat each piece of eggplant with flour, shaking off the excess.

3 Pour just enough olive oil in a jelly-roll pan or other shallow roasting pan to coat the bottom lightly. Place the pan in the oven. When the oil is very hot (sprinkle in some flour—it should sizzle), arrange the eggplant slices in the pan in one layer. Brush a little more olive oil over each piece of eggplant. Bake, turning once, until lightly browned on both sides, 10 to 15 minutes per side. Remove from the oven, and set aside. Reduce the oven temperature to 375°F.

4 Heat a large, heavy skillet over medium-high heat. When it is hot, add the ground beef, and cook, breaking up the meat with the side of a spoon until it is crumbly and no pink remains. With a slotted spoon, remove the meat to a large plate lined with several thicknesses of paper towels. Discard the fat remaining in the skillet, then wipe it with paper towels. Return the meat to the skillet. Over medium-high heat, stir in the onion, garlic, tomatoes, wine, tomato paste, bay leaves, cinnamon stick, and cheesecloth packet of allspice. Reduce the heat, and simmer, uncovered, until most of the liquid has been absorbed or evaporated, 30 to 35 minutes. Remove the bay leaves, cinnamon stick, and allspice. Season with salt and pepper.

5 To assemble the *moussaka*, arrange the eggplant slices in a single layer in the bottom of the prepared baking dish. Sprinkle evenly with ¼ cup of the *graviera* and the parsley. Spoon the meat sauce over the cheese, spreading it evenly, and set aside.

6 Prepare the Béchamel Sauce: In a large, heavy saucepan, heat the butter until bubbly over medium heat. Stir in the flour until the mixture bubbles. Remove the pan from the heat, and whisk in the milk all at once. Return the pan to medium heat and cook, whisking constantly, until the mixture bubbles. Reduce the heat slightly, and cook, stirring constantly with a whisk, for about 10 minutes. The mixture should be very thick. Remove from the heat and stir in the salt, nutmeg, and pepper until well blended. In a small bowl, beat the eggs until well blended. Stir a big spoonful of the hot milk mixture into the eggs to temper them, then whisk the egg mixture into the milk mixture until well blended.

7 Immediately pour the sauce over the ingredients in the baking dish, smoothing the top with the back of a spoon. Sprinkle evenly with ground nutmeg and then the remaining ¼ cup of cheese.

8 Bake for about 25 minutes until hot through. Set aside for about 15 minutes before cutting into servings.

Cabbie: **Steve Kosefas**

Country of Origin: Greece

Other Recipes:

Arnaki Fornou: Greek-Style Roast Leg of Lamb (see page 48)

Avgolemono: Greek Egg and Lemon Soup with Chicken (see page 95)

Tomatoes Stuffed with Chopped Lamb and Rice

"We eat a lot of tomatoes in Greece," Steve says. "The summers are long and hot, perfect for many, many tomatoes. Just make sure that the vine-ripened tomatoes you choose to use for this are firm, or they will split, spilling out the filling. But even if this happens," he adds, "the results will still be delicious, just not as pretty."

Makes 6 servings

6 firm ripe tomatoes, each weighing 8 to 10 ounces

4 tablespoons extra-virgin olive oil

1 pound ground lamb or beef (not too lean; 80 percent lean is about right)

1 large yellow onion, chopped (about 1 cup)

¾ cup raw converted rice, cooked according to package directions for firmer rice

½ teaspoon salt

Pinch freshly ground nutmeg

Freshly ground black pepper, to taste

1 cup chicken broth (see page 92)

1 Hollow out the tomatoes (see Note, page 122), discarding the seeds, but reserving the pulp. Chop the pulp into small pieces and set aside. Turn the tomatoes upside down on paper towels to drain.

2 Position a rack in the center of the oven. Preheat the oven to 350°F.

3 Add 2 tablespoons of the oil to a large skillet set over medium-high heat. When it is hot, add the ground lamb or beef, and cook, stirring and breaking up the meat with the side of a spoon until most of the pink has disappeared. Stir in the onion, and continue to cook, stirring, until the onion is softened, about 3 minutes. Stir in the reserved tomato pulp, cooked rice, salt, nutmeg, and pepper. Cook, stirring frequently, until the mixture is well blended and any liquid that has accumulated in the pan has been absorbed by the rice, about 3 minutes. Remove from the heat, and set aside until cool enough to handle.

4 In a shallow baking pan just large enough to hold the tomatoes comfortably, add the chicken broth, and stir in the remaining 2 tablespoons of oil. Stuff the tomatoes with the ground-beef mixture, mounding it and dividing evenly. Arrange the tomatoes in the baking pan. Bake for 30 to 40 minutes, basting with the pan juices occasionally until the filling is hot and the tomatoes are soft, but not falling apart.

Cabbie: **Rivka Moskovich**

Country of Origin: Israel

Other Recipes:

Roasted Eggplant Salad (see page 16)

Chicken Baked with Oranges (see page 64)

Glazed Oranges with Mint Syrup (see page 179)

Meat-and-Tomato-Stuffed Eggplant

"Here in America we hardly ever think of eggplant shells for holding stuffing, but they work just as well as bell peppers or tomatoes," says Rivka. "The tender flesh of the eggplant, as part of the stuffing mixture, carries all the delicious flavors of the other ingredients." Rivka suggests that if lamb is not to your taste, ground beef can be substituted. The most important thing is to handle the meat very gently. Otherwise, because the turkey is very lean, the mixture will clump together and the stuffing will be heavy. "Turkey," she adds, "is very popular in Israel. That surprises a lot of people, who think of turkey as being strictly American."

MAKES 6 SERVINGS

3 purple eggplants, as straight and oval shaped as possible (about 12 ounces each)

4 large tomatoes, peeled, seeded, and coarsely chopped (about 2 cups; see Note)

1¼ teaspoons salt

1 large egg

½ pound ground lamb shoulder

½ pound ground turkey

½ cup (about 12) crushed soda crackers (Saltines)

1 medium-size yellow onion, finely chopped (about ½ cup)

2 large cloves garlic, minced

¼ cup chopped fresh parsley

½ teaspoon freshly ground black pepper

½ teaspoon dried rosemary leaves, crumbled

Hot cooked white rice, for serving

1 Preheat the oven to 350°F. Lightly grease or coat the bottom of a large, glass baking dish with cooking spray. Pull the leaves off the eggplants, but leave the stems intact. Cut the eggplants in half lengthwise. Scoop out the pulp, leaving a ¼-inch-thick shell and reserving the pulp in a large bowl. (A melon baller or a grapefruit spoon works well for this task.)

2 Reserve about ½ cup of the chopped tomatoes. In a medium-size bowl, mix the remaining tomato pieces with the eggplant pulp, along with ½ teaspoon of the salt. Spread this mixture in the bottom of the prepared baking dish. Nestle the eggplant shells into the eggplant mixture.

3 In a large bowl, beat the egg. Add the ground lamb, ground turkey, crushed crackers, onion, garlic, parsley, pepper, rosemary, and the remaining ¾ teaspoon salt. Mix gently with your hands just until well combined. Spoon into the eggplant shells, packing the filling in gently and mounding it slightly. The shells will be quite full. Bake for 45 minutes to 1 hour, or until the eggplant is tender and a meat thermometer inserted in the center of the meat mixture registers 160°F. As the stuffed eggplant shells bake, baste occasionally with the sauce formed by the eggplant-tomato mixture as it accumulates. Serve with hot cooked rice and the remaining sauce.

NOTE: How to Peel, Seed, and Hollow a Tomato—To peel a whole ripe tomato (an under-ripe tomato is almost impossible to peel), with a very sharp knife, cut an X through the skin on the blossom (round) end of the tomato. With a kitchen fork, spear the tomato firmly in the stem end. Submerge the tomato in boiling water for 3 to 10 seconds, or just until the flaps of the X begin to curl up. (The time it takes to loosen the skin depends on the tomato's size and state of ripeness.) Remove from the water and immediately pull or peel off the skin, starting with one of the flaps.

To seed a tomato, cut a peeled or unpeeled tomato in half crosswise or just below the shoulders on the stem end. With your index finger, loosen and coax the seeds out of each section. (To save the juice, do this over a sieve set in a bowl.)

To hollow a tomato, using a serrated knife (a curved grapefruit knife works especially well), cut out the core and then the flesh separating the seed sections, being careful not to puncture the shell.

TAXI TRIVIA: To increase your chances of hailing a cab during peak hours, position yourself at a corner so that you can watch for cabs coming along the avenue, as well as crosstown on the streets.

Cabbie: **Elsayed M. Ramadam**
Country of Origin: Egypt

Other Recipes:

Samak Magly: Fried Porgy (see page 78)

White Beans with Zucchini (see page 153)

Middle Eastern Chopped Salad with Tahini Dressing (see page 162)

"Fasolia"

Beef and Green Bean Casserole

"In my home in Alexandria, this was served as a very quick and simple meal on the days my mother did shopping," Elsayed informs us. "This food is very comforting for me. I eat it with nothing else besides a glass of soda or after-dinner tea."

MAKES 4 SERVINGS

½ pound green beans, trimmed and cut into
  1- to 1½-inch lengths
Salt and freshly ground black pepper, to taste
½ pound ground beef (85 percent lean)
1 medium-size yellow onion, chopped (about ½ cup)
¾ cup water
2 tablespoons tomato paste
Hot cooked white rice or mashed potatoes,
  for serving

1 Preheat the oven to 350°F.

2 Place the beans in the bottom of a 1½-quart casserole. Sprinkle with salt and pepper.

3 In a medium-size skillet set over medium-high heat, cook the ground beef, breaking up the meat with the side of a spoon until almost no pink remains. Spoon the meat evenly over the beans. Season with salt and pepper.

4 In the fat remaining in the skillet (you may have to add just a little oil), cook the onion over medium-high heat, stirring almost constantly, until softened and just starting to brown. Spoon the onion evenly over the beef. Season with salt and pepper. Off the heat, add the water to the skillet, stirring to pick up any crusty, brown bits that cling to the bottom of the pan. Add the tomato paste, and stir until well blended. Drizzle the tomato mixture over the contents in the casserole. Cover, and bake for about 45 minutes, or until hot and bubbly. Serve over cooked white rice or mashed potatoes.

Cabbie: **Kwolk Sin**

Country of Origin: China

Other Recipes:

Beef, Pork, or Shrimp Lo Mein (see page 129)

Stir-fried Pork

Kwolk readily acknowledges that it is not very Chinese to do so, but he likes to "wash down" this stir-fry with a bottle of Budweiser. Chinese Tea (see page 191), he says, would undoubtedly be more traditional.

This is a quick and easy stir-fry using very few ingredients. (Also keep in mind that many supermarkets now carry meat specially cut for stir-fry, thus saving the cook even more time.) Like most stir-fries, this one is very versatile. You can add garlic along with the scallions and ginger, and other vegetables, too, such as snow peas or thinly sliced celery. And, although not called for in the recipe, a few drops of Asian sesame oil stirred in just before serving is highly recommended.

MAKES 4 TO 6 SERVINGS

¼ cup peanut oil

1 pound lean pork or beef, cut for stir-fry

10 scallions, diagonally sliced into ½-inch pieces, including most of the green tops

2-inch piece fresh ginger, peeled and shredded (discard the stringy pieces that collect on the outside of the grater)

¼ cup oyster sauce mixed with 6 tablespoons water

Hot cooked white rice, for serving

1 Heat the oil in a wok or large, heavy skillet over high heat. When the oil is very hot, almost to the point of smoking, add the pork. Cook over high heat, stirring and tossing constantly, just until the pork is cooked through and lightly browned, 3 to 4 minutes. With a slotted spoon, remove the pork to a bowl, and set aside.

2 To the hot oil remaining in the wok, stir in the scallions and ginger, then add the oyster-sauce mixture. Cook over medium-high heat, stirring constantly, until the scallions are barely tender, 2 to 3 minutes. Return the meat to the pan, and stir until heated through. Serve over hot rice.

VARIATION: For variety, toss in a favorite vegetable, such as lightly steamed broccoli, adding it just before you return the meat to the pan in the final step.

Cabbie: **Roberto Fable**

Country of Origin: Puerto Rico

Rice and Beans with Spiced Pork

"When my kids come over and I cook this for dinner, they always say 'Pa, you should open a restaurant.'" Roberto adds that the rice and beans can be served without the pork as a vegetarian main course. "I serve a big salad and a big loaf of bread with this meal."

For this recipe, you will need a large skillet (at least 12 inches in diameter with a 2½- to 3-inch side) with a lid.

MAKES 8 SERVINGS

Rice and Beans

3 tablespoons olive oil

1 small green bell pepper, cored, seeded, and finely chopped (about 1 cup)

1 large yellow onion, chopped (about 1 cup)

2 small boiling potatoes, peeled and finely diced (about 1½ cups)

2 cloves garlic, minced

2 (14½-ounce) cans pink beans, drained into a colander and rinsed

1 (4-ounce) jar diced pimientos, drained and chopped

1 (8-ounce) can tomato sauce

2 tablespoons ketchup

1 cup water

1 teaspoon adobo seasoning (available in the Latin section of most supermarkets)

½ teaspoon crumbled dried oregano

1 cup long-grain rice, cooked as the package directs for firmer rice

Spiced Pork

1 clove garlic, puréed (see Note, page 17)

½ teaspoon adobo seasoning

½ teaspoon crumbled dried oregano

Freshly ground black pepper, to taste

1 pound boneless pork chops, cut into ½-inch cubes

1 tablespoon lard, bacon fat, or solid shortening

1 Prepare the Rice and Beans: In a large, deep skillet, heat the olive oil over medium-high heat. Add the bell pepper, onion, potatoes, and garlic. Cook, covered, stirring often and adjusting the heat as necessary, until the potatoes are tender, about 15 minutes. Stir in the beans, pimientos, tomato sauce, ketchup, water, adobo seasoning, and oregano, then simmer the mixture, uncovered, for 15 minutes, stirring occasionally.

2 While the bean mixture is simmering, prepare the Spiced Pork: In a small bowl, mix together the puréed garlic, adobo seasoning, oregano, and pepper; set aside.

3 Pat the pork cubes dry with paper towels. Heat the lard in a large, heavy skillet over high heat. When it is very hot, add the pork, and cook, stirring and turning frequently, until the cubes are crusty brown and no trace of pink remains in the centers, about 10 minutes. Sprinkle the spice mixture over pork, and stir, tossing, until the spices are evenly distributed and very fragrant, about 20 seconds. With a slotted spoon, remove the pork cubes from the skillet, and drain on paper towels. Stir the rice into the bean mixture until all the ingredients are evenly blended and the mixture is hot. Stir in the pork cubes until well blended. Serve immediately in large, shallow bowls.

Cabbie: **Mirza Baig**

Country of Origin: Pakistan

"Murghi"

Pakistani Chicken Skillet Supper

Chicken parts other than breasts can be used to make *murghi*. As a matter of fact, we preferred to use either whole drumsticks and thighs or a mixture of both, since dark meat stands up better to stewing than breasts, which tend to become a little dry and stringy when stewed.

"We always serve *murghi* with *roti*, a flat bread we favor in Pakistan. Actually, we serve almost everything with flat bread. The tool we use to make it is called a *tava*, but all flat breads can be cooked in a skillet or on a griddle. Also, flat breads are easy to buy in Middle Eastern grocery stores, and they taste nearly as good as homemade."

The *roti* that Mirza refers to is almost identical to *Chapati* (see page 171), which is easy and kind of fun to make. "As the lady in the Indian grocery store said to us: '*Chapati*, *roti*, it's the same.'"

MAKES 4 TO 6 SERVINGS

---

4 bone-in chicken breast halves (about 2 pounds total)

Salt and freshly ground black pepper

All-purpose flour

2 tablespoons olive or vegetable oil

1 large yellow onion, chopped (about 1 cup)

4 cloves garlic, minced

2 medium-size tomatoes, cored, seeded, and chopped (see Note, page 122)

1 cup chicken broth (see page 92)

1 cup water

2 cups cut green beans, fresh, or frozen and thawed

2 to 3 cups hot cooked white rice

1 Use a large, heavy knife or meat cleaver to chop each breast half crosswise into 3 pieces, or ask the meat person to do this for you. Season lightly with salt and pepper, and dust with flour.

2 Heat the oil in a large skillet over high heat. When it is hot, add the breast pieces, skin-side down, and cook, turning, until golden brown, adjusting the heat as necessary. With tongs, remove the chicken to a plate and set aside.

3 Stir the onion and garlic into the drippings remaining in the skillet and cook over medium heat, stirring almost constantly, until the onion is softened and just starting to brown, about 8 minutes. Add the tomato and cook, stirring, 2 to 3 minutes longer. Stir in the chicken broth and water. Return the chicken, skin-side up, to the skillet, along with any juices that have accumulated on the plate, and bring to a simmer. Cover, and simmer for about 20 minutes, basting the chicken with the pan juices two or three times.

4 When the chicken is fork-tender, stir in the beans, and continue to cook, uncovered, until the beans are tender, about 8 minutes. Add the rice, and stir until heated through. Ladle into warm, shallow soup bowls, dividing the chicken pieces evenly. (If you prefer, spoon a generous mound of warm rice into each soup plate, and spoon the chicken mixture over it.)

Cabbie: **Gabriel Parada**
Country of Origin: Colombia

"Arroz con Pollo"
Spanish Chicken with Rice

"There are as many versions and slight variations of this traditional Spanish dish as there are cooks who make it," says Gabriel. "This is how it has always been done in my family.

"My mother uses dark chicken parts rather than a whole chicken. She says dark chicken stays juicier."

This is a wonderful recipe, a dish that is perfect for a party, since it can be completely assembled and then baked during pre-dinner drinks. Serve with a big salad of many components and a good, crusty bread and there you have it.

A shallow skillet is too small to fit all the ingredients. You will need a large, deep skillet (about 12 inches in diameter with a 2½- to 3-inch side) with a lid. A large Dutch oven can also be used.

MAKES 8 TO 10 SERVINGS

---

3 ½ pounds broiler-fryer chicken parts, preferably drumsticks, thighs, and wings with the tips removed

Salt and freshly ground black pepper, to taste

¼ cup olive oil

½ teaspoon crumbled saffron

3 cups hot chicken broth (see page 92)

1 large yellow onion, cut in half through the stem and the halves cut into thin vertical slices (about 1 cup)

2 cups raw converted white rice

3 cloves garlic, minced

1 (14½-ounce) can undrained diced tomatoes

1 (4-ounce) can diced or sliced pimientos, drained

1 cup fresh or frozen peas

1 cup chorizo sausage slices (about 5 ounces), or dry,
  spicy salami slices
½ teaspoon ground cumin
2 hard-cooked large eggs, sliced
½ to 1 cup halved pimiento-stuffed olives

1 Preheat the oven to 350°F.

2 Season the chicken pieces with salt and pepper. Heat the oil in a very large, deep skillet or Dutch oven over medium-high heat. When the oil is very hot, add the chicken pieces, and cook, turning the chicken and adjusting the heat as necessary, until golden on all sides. With tongs, remove the chicken to plate, and set aside. Stir the saffron into the chicken broth, and set aside.

3 To the oil and drippings remaining in the pan, stir in the onion and rice. Cook over medium-high heat, stirring constantly, until the onion is soft and the rice is golden, 3 to 5 minutes. Stir in the garlic, and cook until softened, about 1 minute more. Stir in the chicken broth, undrained tomatoes, pimiento, peas, chorizo, cumin, and ¼ teaspoon pepper until well combined. Arrange the chicken pieces over the rice mixture. Cover, and bake for 1 to 1¼ hours, until the chicken is fork tender.

4 Serve directly from the cooking pan, or spoon onto a large serving platter. Garnish with the egg slices and olives.

TAXI TRIVIA: The earnings of a cab driver varies from $250 a week to $1,500 a week, depending on the aggressiveness of the driver.

Cabbie: **Kwolk Sin**
Country of Origin: China

Other Recipes:

Stir-fried Pork (see page 124)

Beef, Pork, or Shrimp Lo Mein

When he gave us this recipe, Kwolk advised us that the vegetables he suggests can easily be replaced with asparagus, celery, snow or sugar peas, mung-bean sprouts, leeks, bok choy, mushrooms (fresh or dried), canned bamboo shoots, baby corn, straw mushrooms, or water chestnuts, for example. "When you go to make stir-fry," he says, "have everything ready at your elbow, so all you have to do is keep adding things to the wok."

Those of us who consider convenience foods a latter-day invention should be reminded that the Chinese have been making their own version of fast food for centuries: stir-fries. To make this classic stir-fry go even more rapidly, use precut vegetables and meat—easy to find at most supermarkets.

MAKES 4 TO 6 SERVINGS

¼ pound green beans, trimmed and cut into 1-inch lengths (about 1 heaping cup)

1 small red bell pepper, cored, seeded, and cut into thin strips (about 1 heaping cup)

¼ pound tiny broccoli florets (about 1 heaping cup)

¾ pound fresh, thin-cut Chinese egg noodles, or 1 (10-ounce) package dry Chinese egg noodles (see Note, below)

2 tablespoons Asian sesame oil

4 tablespoons peanut oil

½ to ¾ pound boneless beef or pork, cut for stir-frying, or ¾ pound small shrimp, peeled and deveined

1-inch piece fresh ginger, peeled and minced

2 cloves garlic, minced

8 scallions, trimmed and cut into 1-inch lengths, including some of the green tops (about 1 cup)

1 cup chicken broth (see page 92)

1 tablespoon oyster sauce

2 tablespoons soy sauce

2 tablespoons cornstarch

1 Fill a large saucepan with lightly salted water and heat to a boil. Add the green beans, bell pepper, and broccoli and cook just until slightly tender, about 5 minutes. Remove the vegetables with a slotted spoon, drain in a colander, rinse with cold water, and set aside. Do not pour out the boiling water.

2 In the same pan, cook the fresh noodles in the boiling water for 3 minutes. (Cook dry noodles or angel hair pasta as the package directs.) Drain the noodles in a colander, then rinse with cold water. When well drained, toss with the sesame oil, and set aside.

3 Heat 2 tablespoons of the peanut oil over high heat in a wok or large, heavy

skillet. When the oil is very hot and shimmering, add the meat, and cook, stirring frequently, just until cooked through, about 2 minutes. (If using shrimp, stir-fry just until pink and firm.) Remove with a slotted spoon to a bowl, and set aside.

4 Add another tablespoon of oil to the wok over high heat. When it is very hot, stir in the ginger and garlic, and cook until very fragrant, about 30 seconds. Add the green beans, bell pepper, broccoli, scallions, and ½ cup of the chicken broth. Cook, stirring, until the vegetables are crisp-tender, 2 to 3 minutes. With a slotted spoon, remove the vegetables to the bowl containing the meat or shrimp, and set aside.

5 In a small bowl, whisk together the oyster and soy sauces, cornstarch, and the remaining ½ cup of chicken broth until smooth. Add the remaining tablespoon of oil to the wok over high heat. When it is very hot, add the cooked noodles, and cook, stirring, until hot. Return the vegetables and meat or shrimp to the wok. Stir the cornstarch mixture into the noodle mixture, and continue to cook, stirring, until the sauce has thickened slightly and the mixture is heated through. Turn onto a large platter and serve immediately.

NOTE: Defining Lo Mein—*Lo mein* is the Chinese term for egg noodles. They are available both fresh and dried, although fresh is definitely preferable. Fresh lo mein, either thin- or thick-cut, can be found in the refrigerated section of Chinese grocery stores. The thick-cut variety is used most often to make cold noodle salads. The dried variety is easy to find in the Asian foods section of most supermarkets, but if push should come to shove, fresh or dried angel hair pasta, or fresh or dried linguine can be used.

BIG APPLE BITE: Ellis Island Immigration Station officially opened its doors to the world on Friday, January 1, 1892. Annie Moore, a fifteen-year-old Irish girl, was the first to be questioned in the immigration station's second-floor Registry Room.

Cabbie: **Wilson Eng**
Country of Origin: China

Other Recipes:

Jing-Sting Ho: Steamed Oysters with Garlic-and-Ginger Sauce (see page 25)

Fried Rice with Egg

"It's simple to change this dish by adding two cups of cooked diced shrimp or chicken instead of egg," says Wilson. "If you have a Chinese grocery store where you live, you can sometimes get a nice piece of seasoned and cooked roast pork, all ready to cut into little pieces, and then you can have 'roast pork and fried rice,' which I know is a real American favorite."

MAKES 4 SERVINGS

2 cups long-grain converted white rice, rinsed
Salt
¼ cup oyster sauce
2 tablespoons light Japanese soy sauce
3 large eggs, beaten just until blended
2 tablespoons peanut or vegetable oil
1 cup frozen baby peas, thawed
2 or 3 scallions, thinly sliced, including some of the
    green tops (⅓ to ½ cup)

1 At least a day before you plan to make the fried rice, place the rinsed rice in a heavy, medium-size saucepan. Add 4 cups of cold water and salt to taste. Bring to a boil over high heat. Cover, and cook at a gentle boil until the water has cooked down to the level of the rice. With a spoon (not a fork), stir the rice well. Cover, and reduce the heat to low. Continue to cook for about 15 minutes, or until the rice is tender. Fluff with a fork. Cool to room temperature before covering and refrigerating for 24 hours.

2 Break up any clumps of the cold rice with your fingers and set aside. In a small bowl, stir together the oyster sauce and soy sauce, and set aside.

3 Coat a large, nonstick skillet with non-stick vegetable spray and set over medium-high heat. When the skillet is hot, add the eggs, swirling them around to make sure they coat the whole bottom of the pan. Cook, without stirring, and adjusting the heat as necessary, until the eggs are firm and cooked through but not yet starting to brown lifting the skillet and tilting it so that the eggs cook evenly. Slide the eggs onto a plate and when they have cooled cut into small pieces and set aside.

4 Return the skillet to the burner, and heat the oil over high heat. When it is hot, add the peas and scallions, and cook, stirring constantly, until the scallions are limp, about 1 minute. Stir in the rice, sauce mixture, and eggs until well mixed. Continue to cook, stirring, until the rice is heated through, 1 to 2 minutes.

Cabbie: **Yazid Anes**

Country of Origin: Algeria

Other Recipes:

Roasted Peppers with Vinaigrette (see page 18)

Carrot Salad (see page 160)

"Checkouka"

A Skillet Meal of Eggs, Roasted Peppers, and Tomatoes

"This easy supper is like a frittata," says Yazid. "Sometimes I add a few pieces of spicy sausage (something suggested to me by an American friend), which is very good. I suggest you eat this with French bread or warm pita bread."

MAKES 6 TO 8 SERVINGS

1 red bell pepper

1 green bell pepper

6 large eggs

1 teaspoon salt

2 tablespoons olive oil

3 cloves garlic, minced

4 medium-size tomatoes, peeled, seeded, hollowed (see Note, page 122), and chopped (about 3 cups) or 2 (14½-ounce) cans undrained diced tomatoes

1 Roast the peppers, and cut them into strips as instructed in Roasted Peppers with Vinaigrette (see page 18), and set aside. Preheat the oven broiler.

2 In a medium-size bowl, beat the eggs with the salt just until well mixed but not frothy, and set aside. Heat the oil in a large, ovenproof skillet over medium-high heat. When it is hot, add the garlic, and cook briefly, stirring, just until softened, about 1 minute. Stir in the tomatoes, and cook, covered, until the tomatoes have given up most of their juice, about 10 minutes. (If using canned tomatoes, merely bring the mixture to a simmer.) Add the roasted pepper strips, and continue to cook, stirring frequently, until most of the liquid from the tomatoes has evaporated.

3 Pour the beaten eggs over the tomato mixture. Continue to cook without stirring just until the eggs are set around the edges. Immediately transfer the skillet to the oven. Broil until the eggs are just set on top, about 5 minutes. Be careful not to overcook. To serve, cut into 6 or 8 wedges.

Cabbie: **Vidhu Bhushan**
Country of Origin: Kashmir

"Kofta"
Lotus Root Balls with Spicy Tomato Sauce

"When you make these balls, be sure to pack them firmly," advises Vidhu. "But when you fry them, they must be handled very gently or they may fall apart. Steamed spinach or a green salad is very good with this. Fruit juice is what we drink with every meal."

The root of the water lotus, as well as the leaves and seeds, are all used extensively in Asian and Middle Eastern cooking. Occasionally the roots can be found fresh in Asian markets, although canned lotus root is much easier to locate, most often in ethnic markets that cater to a Middle Eastern clientele. The flavor of lotus root is pleasantly flowery with a texture similar to hearts of palm.

MAKES 4 SERVINGS

1 (14-ounce) can lotus root, drained and rinsed

1 medium-size yellow onion, minced (about ½ cup)

2 cloves garlic, minced

2-inch piece fresh ginger, peeled and minced

1 teaspoon all-purpose flour

1¼ teaspoons garam masala (available in Middle Eastern markets)

⅛ teaspoon freshly ground black pepper

¼ cup vegetable oil

2 tablespoons regular sour cream

1 (14½-ounce) can undrained diced tomatoes

½ teaspoon turmeric

1 small chile pepper, seeded and minced (optional)

1 cup water

1 tablespoon chopped cilantro

Hot steamed couscous, cooked according to package directions, for serving

1 In a food processor, purée the lotus root. In a medium-size bowl, mix the purée with half the onion, half the garlic, half the ginger, the flour, ¼ teaspoon of the garam masala, and the pepper until very well blended. Scoop the mixture out of the bowl by measuring tablespoonsful, and roll into firm balls. You should have between 16 and 18 balls.

2 Heat the oil in a large skillet over high heat. When it is hot, add the lotus root balls, and cook over medium heat, turning the balls and adjusting the heat as necessary, until they are dark brown and crusty on all sides. With a slotted spoon, remove the balls from the skillet to a plate and set aside.

3 Stir the remaining onion into the hot oil left in the skillet. Cook over medium heat, stirring, until the onion is very soft, about 5 minutes. Stir in the remaining garlic and ginger. Cook, stirring, just until the garlic and ginger are very fragrant, about

30 seconds. Stir in the remaining teaspoon of garam masala, the sour cream, undrained tomatoes, turmeric, chile pepper if using, and water until well blended. Bring to a boil, then lower the heat and simmer for about 10 minutes until the mixture is quite thick.

4 Return the lotus root balls to the skillet. Cook, basting the balls with the sauce, for 1 or 2 minutes until they are heated through. Stir in the cilantro, and serve immediately, spooned over freshly steamed couscous.

Cabbie: **Mohammad Rahman**

Country of Origin: Bangladesh

Other Recipes:

Sag Baji: Spinach with Onions and Garlic (see page 151)

Spinach and Tomatoes Wrapped in Flat Bread

"Although most Americans will want to eat this version as a light meal or a snack, in Bangladesh we often add tomatoes, wrap it in a flat bread, and eat it for breakfast. My mom really loves this."

MAKES 4 SERVINGS

3 tablespoons olive oil

1 small yellow onion, minced (about ¼ cup)

2 (10-ounce) bags fresh spinach, tough stems removed, rinsed, drained, and dried

1 (14½-ounce) can diced tomatoes, well drained

3 cloves garlic, minced

¼ teaspoon salt

Freshly ground black pepper, to taste

1 recipe *Chapati* (see page 171), for serving

1 Heat the oil in a Dutch oven or other large, heavy saucepan. When it is very hot, add the onion, and cook over medium heat, stirring, until softened, 3 to 5 minutes. Add the spinach by the handful, stirring rapidly just until it wilts down enough to add the next handful. Stir in the tomatoes, garlic, salt, and pepper. Continue to cook over medium-low heat, stirring, for a few moments until most of the steaming has stopped.

2 To serve, spoon the mixture down the center of a warm *Chapati* (see page 171), then fold over the sides to make a flat packet.

Cabbie: **Joseph Bernard**

Country of Origin: France

Other Recipes:

Baked Shrimp à la Française (see page 86)

French Vegetable-Beef Soup (see page 90)

Sausage and Apples, Normandy Style

Calvados is the famous apple brandy from Normandy. A well-stocked liquor store will generally have it on hand, but you can substitute applejack brandy (or even a good, fresh apple cider). "I can buy *boudin blanc* in many places in New York," Joseph says, "but depending on where you live, it may not be so easy for you. If I had to substitute, I suppose I would use *bockwurst*, which is a similar, delicately flavored German veal sausage. Potatoes mashed with butter and cream is what we always eat with this."

MAKES 4 SERVINGS

3 or 4 links (about 1 pound) fresh French white sausage (**boudin blanc**) or **bockwurst**, cut into ¾-inch slices

4 small Granny Smith or other firm, tart apples (about 1½ pounds), peeled, cored, halved, and cut into ¼-inch crosswise slices

Ground cinnamon

¼ cup Calvados, applejack, or good apple cider

¼ cup heavy cream

Chopped fresh parsley, for garnish

1 Preheat the oven to 350°F. In a large, cold skillet, arrange the sausage slices in one layer. Set over medium-high heat, and cook, turning the slices once or twice until they are crisp and nicely browned on both sides, about 10 minutes. Remove from the heat and set aside.

2 In a 2-quart casserole, arrange a layer of about one-fourth of the sausage slices. Cover the sausage with a layer of about one-fourth of the apple slices. Sprinkle lightly with cinnamon. Continue in this manner to make 4 layers, ending with the apple slices. Stir the Calvados into the skillet in which the sausage was browned, scraping up any crusty, brown bits that cling to the bottom of the pan. Stir in the cream until well blended. Pour this mixture evenly over the casserole.

3 Cover, and bake for 1 hour until the apples have cooked down and the mixture is bubbling. Sprinkle with parsley before serving.

Cabbie: **Arshad Iqbal**
Country of Origin: Pakistan

Other Recipes:

Kharathi Stewed Chicken (see page 68)

Spiced Rice with Peas (see page 148)

Raita: An Indian Condiment (see page 161)

"Chapli"

Pakistani Ground Beef in Pita Breads

"This is a stew that makes what you Americans call a 'snack' or a 'sandwich,'" Arshad says. "Of course, you can serve it as a stew, if you would like to, with pieces of flat bread (see *Chapati*, page 171) and a salad."

MAKES 4 TO 6 SERVINGS

1½ pounds ground beef (80 to 85 percent lean)

¼ cup **kecap manis** (available in Asian markets and gourmet stores)

1 medium-size yellow onion, finely chopped (about ½ cup)

3 cloves garlic, minced

2-inch piece fresh ginger, peeled and minced

1 serrano chile, seeds and ribs removed, minced

2 teaspoons garam masala (available in Middle Eastern markets)

1 to 2 tablespoons vegetable oil

2 warm pita breads, cut crosswise so that there is a pocket in each half, or 4 **Chapatis** (see page 171)

1 In a large bowl, with a dinner fork, gently mix together the ground beef, *kecap manis*, onion, garlic, ginger, chile, and garam masala until well blended. Cover the surface of the ground-beef mixture with plastic wrap, and set aside for 30 minutes to give the seasonings an opportunity to permeate the meat.

2 Heat the oil in a large, nonstick skillet over high heat. When it is hot, add the ground-beef mixture, and cook over medium-high heat, stirring and breaking up the meat with the side of a spoon, until the mixture is juicy and no pink remains. (Ideally the stew should contain small lumps of meat, so don't break it up completely.) Serve immediately in pita pockets or wrapped in flat bread.

Chapter 6 Appetizers and First Courses Meat and Poultry Fish and Seafood Hearty Soups and Stews Casseroles and Skillet Meals Side Dishes and Salads Breads and Baked Goods Desserts and Other Sweet Things Appetizers and First Courses Meat and Poultry Fish and Seafood Hearty Soups and Stews Casseroles and Skillet Meals Side Dishes and Salads Breads and Baked Goods Desserts and Other Sweet Things Appetizers and First Courses Meat and Poultry Fish and Seafood Hearty Soups and Stews Casseroles and Skillet Meals Side Dishes and Salads Breads and Baked Goods Desserts Other Sweet Things Appetizers and First Courses Meat and Poultry Fish and Seafood Hearty Soups and Stews Casseroles and Skillet Meals Side Dishes and Salads Breads and Baked Goods Desserts Other Sweet Things Appetizers and First Courses Meat and Poultry Fish and Seafood Hearty Soups and Stews Casseroles and Skillet Meals Side Dishes and Salads Breads and Baked Goods Desserts Other Sweet Things Appetizers and First Courses Meat and Poultry Fish and Seafood Hearty Soups and Stews Casseroles and Skillet Meals Side Dishes and Salads Breads and Baked Goods Desserts and Other Sweet Things Appetizers and First Courses Meat and Poultry Fish and Seafood Hearty Soups and Stews Casseroles and Skillet Meals **Side Dishes and Salads** Breads and Baked Goods Desserts and Other Sweet Things Appetizers and First Courses Meat and Poultry Fish and Seafood Hearty Soups and Stews Casseroles and Skillet Meals Side Dishes and Salads Breads and Baked Goods Desserts and Other Sweet Things Appetizers and First Courses Meat and Poultry Fish and Seafood Hearty Soups and Stews Casseroles and Skillet Meals Side Dishes and Salads Breads Baked Goods Desserts and Other Sweet Things Appetizers and First Courses Meat and Poultry Fish and Seafood Hearty Soups and Stews Casseroles and Skillet Meals Side Dishes and Salads Breads and Baked Goods Desserts and Other Sweet Things Appetizers and First Courses Meat and Poultry Fish and Seafood Hearty Soups and Stews Casseroles and Skillet Meals Side Dishes and Salads Breads and Baked Goods Desserts and Other Sweet Things Appetizers and First Courses Meat and Poultry Fish and Seafood Hearty Soups and Stews Casseroles and Skillet Meals Side Dishes and Salads Breads and Baked Goods Desserts and Other Sweet Things Appetizers and First Courses Meat and Poultry Fish and Seafood Hearty Soups and Stews Casseroles and Skillet Meals Side Dishes and Salads Breads and Baked Goods Desserts and Other Sweet Things Appetizers and First Courses Meat and Poultry Fish and Seafood Hearty Soups and Stews Casseroles and Skillet Meals Side Dishes and Salads Breads and Baked Goods Desserts and Other Sweet Things Appetizers and First Courses Meat and Poultry Fish and Seafood Hearty Soups and Stews Casseroles Skillet Meals Side Dishes and Salads Breads and Baked Goods Desserts and Other Sweet Things

BIG APPLE BITE: The island of Manhattan is 13.5 miles long and 2.3 miles across at its widest point. Going cross-town? Call a cab . . .

Cabbie: **Hossens Tarek**
Country of Origin: Egypt

"Bamia"

Okra or Green Beans in Tomato Sauce

This easy side dish can also be served as a vegetarian main dish over rice, egg noodles, or even mashed potatoes, along with a green salad. "The best okra," Hossens informs us, "is not much bigger than a man's thumb" (3 to 4 inches long). Green beans can be substituted for okra and, because they cook in the same amount of time, the two can even be combined in this tasty side dish.

Okra, a small, carrot-shaped pod with fuzzy green skin, comes from North Africa. The flavor will remind you of eggplant and, like eggplant, okra has a special affinity for tomatoes. The vegetable is a favorite throughout the American South, especially in Creole cooking, most notably gumbo. Choose small, crisp pods with bright color. Large pods tend to be tough and fibrous. The season for okra is May through October, and that's the time to enjoy it, although it is available both frozen and canned. Okra is best steamed or boiled just until tender. If cooked too long, it becomes sticky.

MAKES 4 TO 6 SERVINGS

1 pound fresh okra or green beans
2 tablespoons freshly squeezed lemon juice
4 tablespoons (½ stick) butter
1 medium-size yellow onion, minced
  (about ½ cup)
1 (8-ounce) can tomato sauce
½ cup water
3 cloves garlic, minced
1 jalapeño chile, seeded and minced
Salt and freshly ground black pepper, to taste

1 Trim off the stem ends and tips of the okra pods. Cut each pod into 2 or 3 pieces. (If using green beans, trim the tips, and cut each bean into 2 or 3 pieces.) Place the okra and lemon juice in a medium-size saucepan with just enough water to barely cover. Bring to a boil over high heat. Reduce the heat, and simmer, covered, for about 5 minutes, or until the okra is barely tender. Drain in a colander, rinse with cold water, and set aside. (The recipe can be prepared an hour or so ahead up to this point.)

2 Heat the butter in the same saucepan in which the okra was boiled over medium-high heat. When the butter is hot, add the onion, and cook, stirring frequently, until soft and golden, about 5 minutes. Stir in the tomato sauce, water, garlic, and jalapeño, and simmer, stirring occasionally, for 5 minutes. Stir in the okra, and simmer until it is very tender, but still holds its shape, about 5 minutes more. Season with salt and pepper, and serve.

Cabbie: **Walter Slovakowski**

Country of Origin: Ukraine

Other Recipes:

Ukrainian Mashed Potato Pancakes (see page 143)

PROFILE: Walter, a cab driver for thirty years, is now semi-retired and is considering a move to Las Vegas, even though he's not a gambler. "I just enjoy the shows and all the action," and he figures he can always pick up a job driving a cab if he gets bored.

ABOUT NEW YORK/AMERICA: "After all these years, I consider myself a New Yorker, so I don't know what I'd do in some quiet place." One of Walter's greatest pleasures of driving a cab in New York is being able to stop in at grocery stores in various neighborhoods to pick up the special ingredients he needs for a good meal, "especially fresh sauerkraut and really garlicky Polish sausage."

Brown Sauerkraut

Walter's idea of a perfect dinner consists of a roast pork loin with gravy, Ukrainian Mashed Potato Pancakes (see page 143), and this slightly unusual preparation of sauerkraut. "You've never tasted such a meal," he says. Walter suggests substituting kielbasa (Polish garlic sausage) for pork loin, which he does frequently. "With kielbasa, make sure to have a pot of good mustard on the table, too. I would drink beer with this meal, and a good cup of strong American coffee to follow it."

MAKES 6 SERVINGS

2 tablespoons vegetable oil

1 large yellow onion, finely chopped (about 1 cup)

1 large clove garlic, minced

1 tablespoon mild paprika

1 (32-ounce) bag undrained refrigerated sauerkraut

Freshly ground black pepper, to taste

1 Heat the oil in a large skillet over high heat. When the oil is hot, add the onion, and cook over medium heat, stirring frequently, until golden, about 5 minutes. Stir in the garlic, and cook briefly just until softened, about 1 minute. Stir in the paprika until well blended with the onion and garlic. Add the undrained sauerkraut, and mix well. Season with pepper.

2 Cook over medium heat, stirring occasionally, for about 20 minutes, or until the sauerkraut is very soft, lightly browned, and most of the liquid has evaporated. Serve immediately.

Cabbie: **Stanley Marchak**

Country of Origin: United States

Other Recipe:

Sweet-and-Sour Wilted Lettuce (see page 163)

PROFILE: Stanley describes himself as one of the few remaining old-time cab drivers, who has been behind the wheel for forty-two years and claims to know almost every street and avenue in the five boroughs. Stanley was born in Brooklyn. "Both of my parents emigrated to the United States," says Stanley. "My mother was Polish, and my father was Russian, which made for plenty of good cooking." The genial driver has been married to his wife, Patricia, for as long as he's been driving a cab.

BEING A CABBIE: He drove nights for sixteen years and was never robbed. When he switched to driving the day shift, he was robbed three times. Luckily he was never hurt—he just handed over the money.

MEMORABLE FARES: Stanley has driven many celebrities including Jack Palance, Jimmy Durante, and Frank Sinatra, who he recalls driving to Jilly's, a jazz club on West 52nd Street. "Sinatra liked to knock around. Those were the 'Rat Pack' days."

Polish Potato Pancakes

"I like a glass of cold beer with my potato pancakes. And some applesauce and sour cream, too," says Stanley. The pancakes can be served as Stanley suggests, but are also very compatible with meat and gravy. However, Stanley warns, "unless you have a skillet as big as the diamond at the old Ebbets Field, you'll have to make these pancakes in several batches."

MAKES 12 TO 14 PANCAKES;

4 TO 6 SERVINGS

3 large eggs

1 small yellow onion, shredded (about ¼ cup)

1 teaspoon salt

½ teaspoon freshly ground black pepper

2 to 4 baking potatoes (about 2½ pounds)

3 tablespoons all-purpose flour

Vegetable oil

Applesauce, for serving

Sour cream, for serving

1 In a large bowl, beat the eggs until frothy. Stir in the onion, salt, and pepper. Have ready a ⅓-cup dry-measuring cup.

2 Peel the potatoes and place them in a bowl of cold water (to prevent discoloring) until ready to proceed. On a sheet of waxed paper, shred the potatoes, using the large holes on a four-sided grater. As each potato is shredded, mix it into the bowl with the eggs until well blended. Add the flour and mix until just combined.

3 In a large, nonstick skillet or a nonstick stovetop griddle, add just enough oil to coat the bottom, and set over high heat. When the oil is very hot, almost to the point of smoking, add the potato batter by ⅓ measuring-cupsful, making 4 patties and pressing each one down with the bottom of the measuring cup to form a pancake that is about 3 inches in diameter. Fry over medium-high to high heat until the underside is well browned, about 5 minutes. Turn and fry until the other side is browned and the pancake is cooked through, about 5 minutes more. Keep each batch of pancakes warm on a baking sheet in a low (170°F) oven until all the pancakes are fried. Serve immediately with applesauce and sour cream.

Cabbie: **Walter Slovakowski**
Country of Origin: Ukraine

Other Recipes:
Brown Sauerkraut (see page 141)

Ukrainian Mashed Potato Pancakes

"I started making these pancakes as a way to use leftover mashed potatoes," says Walter. "It turned out I liked them so much that I started mashing potatoes just to make pancakes. I usually serve them with my Brown Sauerkraut (see page 141), but often my wife and I just eat the pancakes for dinner, along with some applesauce and sour cream."

MAKES 4 TO 6 SERVINGS

2 or 3 baking potatoes (about 1½ pounds), peeled and cut into equal-size chunks
6 tablespoons butter
¼ cup whole milk
Salt and freshly ground black pepper, to taste
1 large yellow onion, finely chopped (about 1 cup)
1 large egg, beaten
All-purpose flour, for dredging
2 tablespoons vegetable oil
Applesauce, for serving
Sour cream, for serving

1 Place the potato chunks in a large saucepan, and add enough lightly salted water to cover. Set the pan over high heat and bring to a boil. Lower the heat, cover, and simmer until the potatoes are fork-tender, about 20 minutes. Drain the potatoes in a colander and return them to the saucepan. Add about 3 tablespoons of the butter, then cover, and set aside until the butter has melted.

2 With a hand-held electric mixer or a potato masher, mash the potatoes until there are no lumps. Beat in the milk, then season with salt and pepper. (The potatoes should be just slightly dryer than traditional mashed potatoes.) Set aside, uncovered, until the potatoes have come to room temperature, about 1 hour.

3 In a medium-size skillet over high heat, add 1 tablespoon of the remaining butter. When the butter sizzles, add the onion, and cook over medium heat, stirring frequently, until golden, about 5 minutes. Stir the onion into the mashed potatoes until well blended. Stir the egg into the potatoes until well blended. Refrigerate the pan of potatoes until very cold, at least 2 hours. (The potato mixture will stiffen as it cools.)

4 When ready to cook, sprinkle a generous coating of the flour on a sheet of waxed paper. On another sheet of waxed paper, form the potato mixture into a large patty. Cut the patty into 6 equal portions and form each portion into a patty. Dredge both sides of the patties in the flour.

5 Heat the remaining 2 tablespoons of butter and the oil in a large skillet over high heat. When the butter-and-oil mixture is very hot, add the potato patties. Cook, adjusting the heat as necessary, until well browned on both sides and hot through, about 5 minutes on each side. Transfer to paper towels to drain briefly, and serve hot with applesauce and sour cream.

BIG APPLE BITE: Macy's on 34th Street is the world's largest store, covering 2.1 million square feet and stocking about half a million items.

Cabbie: **Dedi Sharif**

Country of Origin: Indonesia

Other Recipes:

Lamb Satay (see page 55)

Cucumber Salad (see page 157)

"Perkedel Jagong"

Fried Corn Cakes

"These fried corn cakes are a little different from what you find here in America," says Dedi. "In the summer my wife uses fresh corn, which she cuts off the cob (she says the kernels should not be too small). In the winter, you can also use frozen corn kernels." These cakes are marvelous for breakfast (without the scallions), especially if you drizzle a little warm syrup over them and add a couple of slices of crisp bacon to the plate.

MAKES 8 CORN CAKES

1 large egg, lightly beaten

1 (15¼-ounce) can whole-kernel corn, well drained in a colander

6 scallions, finely chopped, including about 1 inch of the green tops

1 tablespoon all-purpose flour

½ teaspoon salt

Vegetable oil

1 In a medium-size bowl, beat the egg until frothy. Stir in the drained corn, scallions, flour, and salt. Have ready a ⅓-cup dry-measuring cup.

2 In a large, nonstick skillet or a nonstick stove top griddle, add just enough oil to coat the bottom, and set over high heat. When the oil is very hot, almost to the point of smoking, add the corn batter by ⅓ measuring-cupsful to make 4 cakes. Flatten each cake slightly with the back of the measuring cup. Fry over medium-high to high heat for about 3 minutes, until the underside is lightly browned. Turn, and fry until the other side is lightly browned, about 3 minutes longer. Remove the corn cakes, and keep them warm on a baking sheet in a low (170°F) oven until the remaining cakes are fried.

Cabbie: **Dennis Launer**

Country of Origin: United States

Other Recipes:

Pan-Broiled Mako Shark (or Swordfish) Steaks (see page 80)

Stuffed Cabbage in Sweet Tomato Sauce (see page 114)

Steamed Bok Choy (see page 154)

Gingered New Potatoes

Dennis, a former restaurant cook, created this simple potato dish to accompany his Pan-Broiled Mako Shark (or Swordfish) Steaks (see page 80). The tang of fresh ginger, not generally associated with potatoes, is a very effective flavor adjunct to both the potatoes and the fish.

MAKES 4 SERVINGS

10 small new potatoes (about 1 pound), cut into quarters

Canola oil

1 tablespoon shredded fresh ginger (discard the stringy pieces that collect on the outside of the grater)

Kosher salt, to taste

1 Place the potato quarters in a large saucepan, add enough lightly salted water to cover, and bring to a boil. Reduce the heat, cover, and boil gently until the potatoes are fork-tender, about 15 minutes.

Drain the potatoes and set aside uncovered. (The recipe can be prepared an hour or so ahead of time, up to this point.)

2 Add enough oil to a large skillet set over medium-high heat to cover the bottom generously. When the oil is hot, add the ginger, and cook, stirring, just until the ginger is fragrant, 5 to 10 seconds. Add the potatoes, and fry, turning frequently, until brown and crisp, about 10 minutes. Drain the potatoes briefly on paper towels. Sprinkle with the salt, and serve immediately.

TAXI TRIVIA: It is illegal for a cabbie to drive more than twelve hours in a twenty-four-hour period.

Cabbies: **Anna and Peter Egan**
Country of Origin: Ireland and the United States

Other Recipes:

Glazed Corned Beef with Vegetables (see page 41)
Irish Lamb Stew (see page 106)
Irish Soda Bread (see page 170)
Emerald Isle Trifle (see page 189)

Mashed Potatoes, Carrots, and Parsnips

"We Irish like our root vegetables and we eat a lot of them," Anna says. "This is a mixture that particularly appeals to our American friends. I think they like the touch of sweetness from the carrots and parsnips. Just be sure to cut all of the vegetables into the same-size pieces so that they will be cooked at the same time."

MAKES 6 TO 8 SERVINGS

3 or 4 medium-size baking potatoes (about 1 pound), peeled and cut into even-size chunks
6 to 8 carrots (about 1 pound), trimmed, peeled, and cut into even-size chunks
4 parsnips (about 1 pound), trimmed, peeled, and cut into even-size chunks
2 tablespoons butter
¼ cup heavy cream
Freshly ground black pepper

1 Place the potatoes and carrots in a large saucepan, and add enough lightly salted water to cover. Bring to a full boil over high heat. Reduce the heat, cover, and boil slowly for 5 minutes. Add the parsnips (they will cook more quickly than the potatoes and carrots), and continue to boil until the vegetables are tender, about 15 minutes.

2 With a measuring cup, scoop out ½ cup of the cooking liquid, and set aside. Turn the vegetables into a colander to drain. Return the drained vegetables to the saucepan, and add the butter and reserved cooking liquid. Beat with an electric mixer until the mixture is fairly smooth. (There will be a few small lumps.) Beat in the cream, then season to taste with salt and pepper. Just before serving, set the pan over low heat, and beat constantly until the mixture is hot.

Cabbie: **Arshad Iqbal**

Country of Origin: Pakistan

Other Recipes:

Kharathi Stewed Chicken (see page 68)

Chapli: Pakistani Ground Beef in Pita Breads (see page 136)

Raita: An Indian Condiment (see page 161)

Spiced Rice with Peas

"Be careful not to bite into the whole spices," Arshad warns. Of course, they can be picked out before serving, but Arshad explains that in Pakistan it is more or less traditional for each diner to perform this little task. He recommends serving this spicy rice with *Chapli* (see page 136) and *roti* or *Chapati* (see page 171). A bowl of icy-cold *Raita* (see page 161) would also be a refreshing addition.

MAKES 8 SERVINGS

3 tablespoons vegetable oil

5 whole cloves

5 black peppercorns

2-inch cinnamon stick

4 cardamom seeds

2 cups raw converted white rice

1 tablespoon ground coriander

1 teaspoon ground cumin

½ teaspoon ground turmeric

3 cups water

2 teaspoons salt

1 cup fresh peas, or frozen peas thawed

Tomato wedges, for garnish

1 Heat the oil in a Dutch oven or other large, heavy stew pot over high heat. When the oil is hot, add the cloves, peppercorns, cinnamon stick, and cardamom. Stir for a few seconds until the spices are very aromatic and begin to change color.

Stir in the rice, coriander, cumin, and turmeric, and cook over medium heat for several minutes, or until the rice is well coated with the oil and ground spices. Stir in the water and salt, and bring to a boil.

2 Cover tightly, and cook at barely a simmer for about 20 minutes, or until the rice is soft and most of the water has been absorbed. Uncover the pot, and sprinkle the peas evenly over the rice. Quickly recover, and cook for about 5 minutes until the peas are hot and tender. Remove from the heat and set aside for 5 minutes before serving.

3 To serve, mix the rice and peas together, and spoon onto a platter. Garnish with the tomato wedges.

Cabbie: **Mohammed Akbar**

Country of Origin: Afghanistan

Other Recipes:

Lamb Shanks with Rice Palau and Yogurt Chutney (see page 51)

Perfectly Cooked Basmati Rice

"You can use the directions on the package to cook basmati rice, but this is so much better, you will eat too much," says Mohammed. "This recipe for rice is the main part of what we eat in Afghanistan. The rest is stews or slowly cooked meat, like my mother's Lamb Shanks with Rice Palau and Yogurt Chutney (see page 51), which I hope you will try."

Makes about 3 cups; 4 servings

1 cup raw basmati rice
1½ cups water
½ teaspoon salt
2 tablespoons butter

1 In a medium-size bowl, soak the rice in cold water to cover by 1 inch or so for 2 hours, then drain in a fine-mesh sieve.

2 Preheat the oven to 500°F.

3 Place the rice in a Dutch oven or other large, heavy, ovenproof pan. Stir in 1 cup of the water and the salt. Bring to a boil, then reduce the heat so that the mixture barely simmers. Cook, uncovered, for 4 to 5 minutes. After 4 minutes, check the rice by rubbing a few grains between your fingers to see if the consistency is such that the grains could be cut with a knife. (This is similar to al dente when cooking pasta.) Drain the rice in a sieve, then rinse it well under lukewarm water and drain again.

4 Return the rice to the same pan in which it was cooked. In a small skillet, heat the butter until bubbly. Stir the hot butter into the rice. Shape the rice into a mound, leaving a space all around the rice in the bottom of the pan. Pour the remaining ½ cup of water *around* the rice, not over it.

5 Cover the pan tightly, and place it in the oven for 10 minutes. Turn off the oven and leave the pot for an additional 10 minutes. Remove the rice from the oven, uncover, and fluff with a fork. It will be perfectly cooked, with each grain puffy and separate.

Cabbie: **Zafar Iqbal**
Country of Origin: Pakistan

PROFILE: Zafar's emigration to the United States seems a bit of a puzzlement. The eloquent cab driver is college educated and was trained as a petroleum technician. "Americans take so much for granted," he says, shaking his head. "You believe that if a person can make a good living somewhere else in the world, why come here? I will tell you why in one word: freedom. Especially religious freedom."

In the ten years since he arrived in this country, Zafar has amassed four medallions (a license to operate a cab in New York City), an admirable accomplishment, considering that each medallion costs roughly the same as a two-bedroom house. "We Pakistanis like to be our own bosses. We are hard working and very family oriented."

BEING A CABBIE: He prides himself, as well as his fellow countrymen, in being scrupulously honest. "Once I found a bag in my cab with twelve thousand dollars in it. I was almost sure I dropped the person who left it at the New York Athletic Club. It's a long story, but I did manage to return the money." More routinely, he says, passengers often don't realize what bill they give you, or two will stick together. "I always give my fares the right change."

Basmati Rice Palao

"It is always surprising to me that my new American friends are not more courageous about flavoring and adding things to rice. In Pakistan, a recipe like this one is often the main meal, but here I find it is very good with simple American food, like roasted chicken. *Raita* (see page 161) and mango chutney would taste good with it too. "We soak rice before we cook it," says Zafar. "That makes it cook faster and rinses off some of the starch, which keeps the grains separate. You must remember also that in the Middle East, rice is not always as clean as your packaged rice, so soaking and rinsing also washes away any dust or debris."

MAKES 6 TO 8 SERVINGS

1 cup raw basmati rice

2 tablespoons vegetable oil

1 large yellow onion, chopped (about 1 cup)

1 teaspoon salt

1 teaspoon whole cumin seeds, or substitute
  ½ teaspoon ground cumin

½ teaspoon ground cardamom

2-inch cinnamon stick, broken in half

2 or 3 medium-size tomatoes (about 1 pound),
  seeded and chopped (see Note, page 122)

1½ cups water

1½ cups frozen peas, thawed

1 Place the rice in a fine-mesh sieve, and rinse with cold water until the water runs clear. In a medium-size bowl, soak the rice in water for 15 minutes. Drain in the sieve, and set aside.

2 Heat the oil in a Dutch oven or other

large, heavy stew pot with a tight-fitting lid over high heat. When the oil is hot, add the onion, and cook over medium heat, stirring, just until the onion is starting to soften, 3 to 5 minutes. Stir in the salt, cumin seeds, cardamom seeds, and cinnamon. Continue to cook, stirring, until the spices become very aromatic, 1 to 2 minutes. Stir in the tomatoes until well blended and softened, 1 to 2 minutes. Add the rice, and cook, stirring, for 3 minutes, or until the rice is very hot. Stir in the water and bring to a boil.

3 Cover, and cook over medium-low to low heat for 10 minutes. (The lid must fit very tightly. If not, cover the pan first with a piece of aluminum foil.) Uncover, and quickly stir in the peas until blended with the rice. Cover, and cook 5 minutes longer. Remove the pan from the heat. Do not uncover. Set aside to steam for 5 minutes before serving.

Cabbie: **Mohammed Rahman**
Country of Origin: Bangladesh

Other Recipes:

Spinach and Tomatoes Wrapped in Flat Bread (see page 134)

"Sag Baji"
Spinach with Onions and Garlic

"In my country, we would eat just this as a simple meal with nothing more than flat bread," says Mohammed, "but here I can understand that you would want to serve it with grilled meat or chicken. It is very healthy and delicious. I have never served it in my home to my American friends when they have not begged for the recipe."

Makes 4 servings

---

3 tablespoons olive oil
1 small yellow onion, minced (about ¼ cup)
2 (10-ounce) bags fresh spinach, tough stems
  removed, washed and drained dry
3 or 4 cloves garlic, minced
¼ teaspoon salt
2 tablespoons freshly squeezed lemon juice
Freshly ground black pepper, to taste

Heat the oil in a large skillet or Dutch oven over high heat. When it is very hot, add the onion, and cook over medium heat, stirring, until softened, 3 to 5 minutes. Add the spinach by the handful, stirring rapidly just until it wilts enough to add the next handful. Stir in the garlic and salt. Continue to cook over medium-low heat, stirring, until most of the steaming has stopped. Remove from the heat, and stir in the lemon juice and pepper. Serve immediately.

Cabbie: **Shahid And Khadim**

Country of Origin: Pakistan

"Dal"

Lentils with Onion and Tomato Sauce

"When I arrived here I was surprised to find that lentils are not very popular in your diet, because in Pakistan we eat them prepared in one of many ways several times a week," Shahid tells us. "This is one of my favorite recipes that I have been eating since I was a boy and I am pleased to share it with you. It will make you think of a thick soup or stew, especially if you add some extra tomatoes and even a little cooked ground beef, and then you can serve it as a main dish, if you like, along with some nice bread and olive oil." If you would prefer this dish to be a little more tomato-y, as Shahid suggests, add another can of tomatoes.

MAKES 8 TO 12 SIDE-DISH SERVINGS;

4 MAIN-DISH SERVINGS

1 (16-ounce) bag brown lentils, rinsed and sorted
as the package directs

4½ cups water

1 teaspoon salt

2 tablespoons vegetable or olive oil

1 large yellow onion, finely chopped (about 1 cup)

1 jalapeño or other hot chile, seeded and minced

2 or 3 cloves garlic, minced

1 (15½-ounce) can undrained diced tomatoes

½ teaspoon garam masala (available in Middle
Eastern markets)

½ cup chopped fresh parsley

1 In a large saucepan, combine the lentils, water, and salt, and bring to a boil over high heat. Reduce the heat, and simmer, covered, until the lentils are tender and most of the water has been absorbed, 25 to 30 minutes.

2 Meanwhile, heat the oil in a large skillet over high heat. When it is hot, add the onion and chile pepper, and cook over medium heat, stirring frequently, until the onion is very soft and starting to brown, about 8 minutes. Stir in the garlic, and continue to cook and stir just until the garlic has softened, about 1 minute. Stir in the undrained tomatoes and garam masala.

3 Add this mixture to the lentils, and cook, stirring, until heated through. Stir in the parsley and serve immediately. (This recipe can be made 1 or 2 hours ahead of serving. In that case, stir in a little water before reheating.)

Cabbie: **Elsayed M. Ramadam**

Country of Origin: Egypt

Other Recipes:

Samak Magly: Fried Porgy (see page 78)

Fasolia: Beef and Green Bean Casserole (see page 123)

Middle Eastern Chopped Salad with Tahini Dressing (see page 162)

White Beans with Zucchini

"In the summer, when I don't have a fare and I am driving past one of the many outdoor markets, I stop and buy vegetables," says Elsayed. "These markets are a lot like the ones in Alexandria where we buy most of our food. When the little zucchinis are on the stands, I buy many of them, and some I use to make this recipe with beans, which is from my mother. She loved good food and she loved to cook. She taught us like crazy, **even the boys**," Elsayed says proudly. "She used a lot of parsley to decorate. You will like this recipe, because you can make it fast when you get home from work, and it will be ready in just a little more than one hour. I like hot cheese on top, so I use more than my mother did, sometimes as much as a cup."

MAKES 4 TO 6 SERVINGS

3 small zucchini (about 1 pound)

Salt and freshly ground black pepper, to taste

2 small yellow onions, thinly sliced and the slices separated into rings (about ½ cup)

1 (15½-ounce) can white beans, drained and rinsed

1 (8-ounce) can tomato sauce

½ cup water

¼ to ½ cup grated Parmesan cheese

1 Preheat the oven to 350°F. Wash and trim the zucchini, then cut into ¼-inch slices. Place the zucchini slices in a lightly greased, 2-quart casserole. Season with salt and pepper. Arrange the onion rings over the zucchini. Spread the beans over the onion slices. Season the beans with pepper. In a small bowl, stir together the tomato sauce and water. Pour evenly over the beans.

2 Cover, and bake for 1 hour. Uncover, and sprinkle evenly with the cheese. Continue to bake, uncovered, for about 10 minutes, or until the cheese is melted.

Cabbie: **Dennis Launer**
Country of Origin: United States

Other Recipes:
Pan-Broiled Mako Shark (or Swordfish) Steaks (see page 80)
Stuffed Cabbage in Sweet Tomato Sauce (see page 114)
Gingered New Potatoes (see page 146)

Steamed Bok Choy

Bok choy is sometimes referred to as Chinese white cabbage, but it should not be confused with Chinese cabbage, which, although closely related, is entirely different. Bok choy comes in bunches—like celery, which it remotely resembles, with wide, pale stems and leafy, bright green tops—and is available year-round in Asian markets and better supermarkets. This versatile vegetable is a popular ingredient in stir-fries, but it can also be served raw in salads, a nice change from the better-known lettuce varieties.

"If you haven't yet discovered bok choy, you'll be glad you did," says Dennis. "Choose bunches of young bok choy that are no longer than 8 to 10 inches, and serve it this way with my Pan-Broiled Shark (or Swordfish) Steaks (see page 80) and Gingered New Potatoes (see page 146)."

MAKES 4 SERVINGS

2 or 3 bunches bok choy (about 1 pound total)
6 to 8 slender scallions, trimmed and cut into ¾-inch
    lengths, including some of the green tops
½ teaspoon salt
2 tablespoons butter
Freshly ground black pepper, to taste

1 Separate the stalks of the bok choy, and trim about 2 inches from the stem ends. Cut the stalks into 1½-inch pieces. In a large bowl, rinse the bok choy in several changes of cold water.

2 Drain the bok choy and place it in a large saucepan, along with any water that clings to the leaves. Add the scallions and salt, and toss together until blended. Set the pan over medium-high heat, and cook, covered, stirring occasionally, until the bok choy is bright green and tender, about 5 minutes. Drain off any remaining water and stir in the butter until it is melted. Turn into a serving dish, and sprinkle generously with pepper.

Cabbie: **Luis Artchabala**

Country of Origin: Ecuador

Other Recipes:

Seco de Pollo: Saffron-flavored Chicken and Vegetables (see page 104)

Cassata: Sicilian Special-occasion Pound Cake (see page 186)

Fried Yuca with Pickled Onion Rings

"Yuca root, when it is fried crisp, is better to me than the best french fries," says Luis. "The pickled onions, one of my mother's inventions, are important to this dish. Don't skip them."

MAKES 4 SERVINGS

1½ pounds yuca root
Kosher salt
Canola oil, for frying
Pickled Onion Rings (recipe follows), for serving

1 Peel the yuca and cut into pieces resembling large french fries. Place in a large saucepan. Cover with lightly salted water, and bring to a boil. Cover, and boil slowly until barely tender, about 3 minutes. Drain in a colander, then arrange in one layer on a baking sheet. Sprinkle the yuca with the salt, turning to coat evenly.

2 Pour the oil into a large skillet to a depth of about ¼ inch. Set the skillet over high heat. When the oil is very hot, carefully slip the yuca into the skillet. Cook over medium-high heat, turning and moving the pieces around, until crisp and golden, about 15 minutes. With a slotted spoon, remove the yuca to paper towels to drain. Transfer to a platter and sprinkle with salt. Scatter the Pickled Onion Rings over the yuca, or serve them on the side.

Pickled Onion Rings

MAKES 4 SERVINGS

2 small red onions,
    cut into very thin slices and the slices
    separated into rings (about 1½ cups)
½ cup red wine vinegar
1 tablespoon sugar
1½ teaspoons salt
¼ teaspoon freshly ground black pepper
¾ cup boiling water

Place the onion rings in a medium-size bowl. In a small bowl, combine the vinegar, sugar, salt, and pepper. Stir in the boiling water until the sugar is dissolved. Immediately pour over the onion rings. Cover, and set aside at room temperature for at least 2 hours or up to 24 hours, stirring the rings occasionally. When ready to serve, drain the onion rings well and arrange them over the fried yuca, or serve them on the side.

Cabbie: **Emmanuel Accimi**
Country of Origin: Haiti

Boiled and Buttered Plantains

"Haitians like meat, but few can afford to eat it every day," says Emmanuel. "Plantains are something we have in abundance. They are healthful and very satisfying, especially when served with rice and beans. In this country, where it seems there is enough money to eat meat at every meal, plantains can be used to make a good side dish instead of potatoes."

Known as "cooking bananas," plantains look like bananas and are, in fact, related, but there most of the similarity ends. Like bananas, plantains ripen off the tree at room temperature and can be refrigerated for a day or two when they are dead-ripe. Plantain flesh is hard, even when completely ripe, and does not develop sweetness as it ripens. They are harder to peel than bananas and are never eaten raw.

Plantains are popular in Latin American countries, where they are often served with rice and beans and generally as a potato substitute. Choose green (under-ripe) plantains, then leave them on the counter and wait until they turn brownish-black.

MAKES 4 TO 6 SERVINGS

3 or 4 plantains (about 2 pounds)
4 tablespoons (½ stick), melted butter
Salt and freshly ground black pepper, to taste

1 Peel the plantains and cut them into ¾-inch slices. Place the slices in a large pot of lightly salted cold water, and bring to a boil. Reduce the heat, and simmer, covered, for about 30 minutes, or until the slices are very tender.

2 Drain the plantain slices, and return them to the cooking pot. Gently stir in the melted butter. Season with salt and pepper and serve immediately.

TAXI TRIVIA: The median age of taxicab drivers is thirty-eight years old.

Cabbie: **Dedi Sharif**
Country of Origin: Indonesia

Other Recipes:

Lamb Satay (see page 55)

Perkedel Jagong: Fried Corn Cakes (see page 145)

Cucumber Salad

"I like to use English cucumbers," says Dedi, "because they have many less seeds and are crisper than regular cucumbers. I think you will like this recipe, because it goes so well with so many things, especially meat cooked outside on a grill."

English cucumbers are readily available and easy to recognize. They are dark green, very long and ridged and, almost without exception, shrink-wrapped in plastic.

The Indonesian rice wine vinegar called for in this recipe is a slightly sweet, mild vinegar, which is very difficult to find, even at ethnic grocery stores. Japanese rice wine vinegar, available in supermarkets everywhere, is an excellent substitute.

MAKES 4 SERVINGS

1 clove garlic, minced

½ small red bell pepper, minced (about ⅓ cup)

¼ cup finely chopped scallion greens

½ cup Indonesian or Japanese rice wine vinegar

Freshly ground black pepper, to taste

1 small English (hothouse) cucumber (about ¾ pound)

1 In a medium-size bowl, combine the garlic, bell pepper, scallion greens, vinegar, and pepper.

2 Rinse the unpeeled cucumber and pat dry. Trim both ends, then slice crosswise as thinly as possible, no more than ⅛ inch thick. (The slicing side on a four-sided grater works well for this.) Stir the cucumber into the vinegar mixture until each slice is well coated with the dressing. Cover, and refrigerate for several hours or overnight, stirring occasionally, before serving.

Cabbie: **David Ghalian**

Country of Origin: Jordan

Other Recipes:

Kofta: Egg-Shaped Meatballs with Tomato Rice (see page 47)

Meloukhiah: Chicken with Chopped Collard Greens and Garlic (see page 69)

"Sarata"

White Bean Salad

If you prefer, you can use dried beans that have been cooked from scratch according to package directions. However, canned beans are very good in this salad and speed things along considerably when you're in a rush.

David serves this salad with *Kofta* (see page 47), although he also recommends enjoying the salad by itself as a light meal, along with a good, hearty bread (see Crusty Country Bread, page 168) to soak up the juices. Obviously, this salad is best when vine-ripened tomatoes are in season, but a 14½-ounce can of drained, diced tomatoes can be substituted when they are not.

MAKES 4 TO 6 SERVINGS

1 (15-ounce) can small white beans

2 medium-size ripe tomatoes, seeded and chopped (see Note, page 122)

1 small red onion, minced (about ½ cup)

¼ cup chopped fresh parsley

¼ cup extra-virgin olive oil

Salt and freshly ground black pepper, to taste

Freshly squeezed lemon juice or red wine vinegar, to taste

1 Drain the beans in a colander and rinse with cold water. Set aside to drain thoroughly.

2 In a large bowl, gently combine the tomatoes, onion, parsley, salt, pepper, olive oil, and a few drops of the lemon juice or vinegar. Add the drained beans, and toss gently until well combined. Turn into a serving bowl, and refrigerate for an hour or so before serving. Adjust the seasonings to taste.

Cabbie: **Nevio Frankovic**

Country of Origin: Yugoslavia

Other Recipes:

Goulash: Yugoslavian Meat Stew (see page 98)

Spinach Salad

"This salad comes from my mother, who was a very good cook," Nevio says. "I like to serve it along with my *Goulash* (see page 98). It is a good recipe to know because it is a little unusual, spinach goes with everything, and almost everybody likes it."

MAKES 4 TO 6 SERVINGS

2 (10-ounce) bags fresh spinach, tough stems removed, rinsed and drained

2 cloves garlic, minced

3 tablespoons vegetable oil

2 teaspoons red wine vinegar

½ teaspoon salt

Freshly ground black pepper, to taste

1 Place the spinach in a large pot with only the water that clings to the leaves. Set over high heat, and cook, turning the spinach from top to bottom almost constantly, just until it has wilted but is still slightly firm, 2 to 3 minutes. With tongs, lift the spinach into a colander to drain.

2 In a medium-size bowl, whisk together the garlic, oil, vinegar, salt, and pepper. Add the spinach and turn gently until well combined. Turn into a serving bowl, and cool to room temperature before serving. The salad can also be refrigerated and served cold.

BIG APPLE BITE: The world's largest globe stands in Queens's Flushing Meadows-Corona Park. The Unisphere is a 700,000-pound steel structure and one of the few remnants of the 1964-65 World Trade Fair.

Cabbie: **Yazid Anes**
Country of Origin: Algeria

Other Recipes:

Roasted Peppers with Vinaigrette (see page 18)

Checkouka: A Skillet Meal of Eggs, Roasted Peppers, and Tomatoes (see page 132)

Carrot Salad

This crunchy salad has just the right flavor, texture, and color to complement grilled or roasted meat or poultry. To save time, though, Yazid suggests substituting 2 cups of packaged shredded carrots for the chopped carrots. "Okay for Americans, but not for Algerians," he adds with a laugh. "There is too much French in us for that!"

MAKES 6 SERVINGS

4 or 5 large carrots, scrubbed and trimmed

1 cup tightly packed fresh parsley sprigs, finely chopped

1 or 2 cloves garlic, finely minced

4 tablespoons Basic Vinaigrette (see page 19)

4 hard-cooked eggs, cut into quarters

18 kalamata olives

1 Cut the carrots in half, then cut each half into lengthwise quarters; cut the quarters into ¼-inch slices. (You should have about 2 cups.)

2 In a medium-size bowl, combine the carrots, parsley, and garlic. Toss with the vinaigrette until well blended. Cover, and refrigerate until ready to serve. Spoon the carrot mixture into the center of a serving platter, and surround with the egg quarters and olives.

BIG APPLE BITE: *Cats* was the longest-running show in Broadway history, having completed over six thousand performances.

Cabbie: **Arshad Iqbal**
Country of Origin: Pakistan

Other Recipes:

Kharathi Stewed Chicken (see page 68)

Chapli: Pakistani Ground Beef in Pita Breads (see page 136)

Spiced Rice with Peas (see page 148)

"Raita"

An Indian Condiment

Arshad recommends serving this creamy condiment with Kharathi Stewed Chicken (see page 68). He explains that *raita* is traditionally served with curries and other spicy dishes as a cooling accent.

Makes about $2\frac{1}{2}$ cups (without cucumber)

1 unwaxed cucumber (optional)

1 (16-ounce) container plain yogurt

1 teaspoon salt

½ teaspoon toasted cumin seeds (see Note), crushed between fingers, or substitute ¼ teaspoon ground cumin

⅛ teaspoon freshly ground black pepper

⅛ teaspoon ground cardamom

1 small onion, minced (about ¼ cup)

1 If using the cucumber, wash it thoroughly and pat dry, but do not peel it. Cut it in half lengthwise, and scoop out the seeds with the tip of a spoon. Shred the cucumber on the large holes of a four-sided grater. (The shredding goes easier if the cucumber is first cut crosswise into two or three lengths and the skin side is shredded first.) Turn the shreds into a colander. Set aside to drain for 1 or 2 hours, stirring occasionally. Before using, gently press down on the shreds with paper towels to remove as much excess liquid as possible.

2 In a medium-size bowl, with a whisk, beat the yogurt for a minute or so until it is creamy and has thickened slightly. Whisk in the salt, cumin seeds, pepper, and cardamom until well blended. Stir in the onion and cucumber, if using. Turn into a serving bowl and refrigerate until serving time. This keeps in an airtight container in the refrigerator for 1 or 2 days.

NOTE: To toast the cumin seeds, place them in a small, cold skillet. Set the skillet over medium-high heat, then shake the pan frequently until the seeds are very aromatic. Remove the skillet from the heat and continue to shake the pan until the seeds have cooled slightly. When cool enough to handle, crumble and crush the seeds between your fingers.

Cabbie: **Elsayed M. Ramadam**
Country of Origin: Egypt

Other Recipes:
Samak Magly: Fried Porgy (see page 78)
Fasolia: Beef and Green Bean Casserole (see page 123)
White Beans with Zucchini (see page 153)

Middle Eastern Chopped Salad with Tahini Dressing

"This salad is so hearty that we often eat it as a main meal with warm flat bread, " Elsayed tells us. "Vegetarians love it. The dressing is so good, and healthful, too, but you must use it soon after it is made, because the oils in the tahini will cause the mixture to separate if it sits for very long."

Tahini is a staple in Middle Eastern cooking. It is a paste made from untoasted sesame seeds that will remind you of natural peanut butter. It is usually sold in cans in specialty and health food stores. Because tahini contains no emulsifiers, it will separate, the solids settling to the bottom of the can and the oil coming to the top. Consequently, tahini needs quite a lot of stirring before it can be used. Do not confuse tahini (typically sold in cans) with Chinese sesame paste (typically sold in jars). The latter is made with roasted sesame seeds and has a completely different flavor.

MAKES 6 TO 8 SERVINGS

Tahini Dressing
2 tablespoons tahini paste, well stirred (available in Middle Eastern markets and better supermarkets)
6 scallions, white and pale green parts only, coarsely chopped (about ½ cup)
1 teaspoon salt
⅛ teaspoon freshly ground black pepper
2 tablespoons red wine vinegar
6 tablespoons extra-virgin olive oil

Salad
1 romaine lettuce heart (the pale green leaf core), finely chopped (5 to 6 cups)
1 cucumber, peeled, seeded, and finely chopped
2 medium-size tomatoes, seeded and finely chopped
½ cup chopped fresh parsley

6 to 8 radishes, finely chopped (about ½ cup)
6 scallions, white parts only, thinly sliced (about ½ cup)

1 Prepare the Tahini Dressing: In a mini food processor or a blender, process the tahini, scallions, salt, pepper, and vinegar. Scrape out of the processor into a medium-size bowl. With a whisk, gradually beat in the olive oil until the dressing is thick and creamy.

2 Prepare the Salad: Toss all of the salad ingredients together in a salad bowl. Add the Tahini Dressing, tossing until well blended, and serve immediately.

Cabbie: **Stanley Marchak**

Country of Origin: United States

Other Recipes:

Polish Potato Pancakes (see page 142)

Sweet-and-Sour Wilted Lettuce

"In our family we've always called this 'salad in a metal bowl'," recalls Stanley. "My mother made it in a metal bowl because, she said, the metal made the lettuce get cold faster. When we have Polish Potato Pancakes (see page 142) we always have this lettuce, too."

To easily remove the core from a head of iceberg lettuce, thump the core end down hard on the kitchen counter, and it will easily twist out. To break apart, lift off the leaves starting at the core end. Tear—don't cut—the leaves into pieces. (The metal knife blade turns the lettuce edges brown.)

MAKES 4 TO 6 SERVINGS

1 head (about 1 pound) iceberg lettuce

1 small yellow onion, cut in half through the stem, and the halves cut into thin vertical slices (optional)

½ cup white vinegar

⅓ cup vegetable oil

1 tablespoon sugar

1 teaspoon salt

¼ teaspoon freshly ground black pepper

2 teaspoons celery seed (optional)

1 Pull off any wilted leaves, and core the lettuce. Pull the head of lettuce apart. Rinse the leaves and drain very well in a colander. Tear the lettuce into bite-size pieces, and place in a large (metal) salad bowl. Add the onion, if using, and toss to combine.

2 In a small microwave-safe bowl, mix together the vinegar, oil, sugar, salt, and pepper. Microwave on high for about 1 minute, or just until very warm. (Alternately, the mixture can be warmed in a small saucepan over medium heat.) Stir to make sure the sugar is dissolved. Stir in the celery seed, if using. Pour the dressing over the lettuce mixture, and toss briefly. Cover and refrigerate until the lettuce is chilled and slightly wilted, about 1 hour.

BIG APPLE BITE: The lower-Manhattan neighborhood Tribeca stands for TRIangle BElow CAnal street.

Chapter 7 Appetizers and First Courses Meat and Poultry Fish and Seafood Hearty Soups and Stews Casseroles and Skillet Meals Side Dishes and Salads Breads and Baked Goods Desserts and Other Sweet Things Appetizers and First Courses Meat and Poultry Fish and Seafood Hearty Soups and Stews Casseroles and Skillet Meals Side Dishes and Salads Breads and Baked Goods Desserts and Other Sweet Things Appetizers and First Courses Meat and Poultry Fish and Seafood Hearty Soups Stews Casseroles and Skillet Meals Side Dishes and Salads Breads and Baked Goods Desserts and Other Sweet Things Appetizers and First Courses Meat and Poultry Fish and Seafood Hearty Soups and Stews Casseroles and Skillet Meals Side Dishes and Salads Breads and Baked Goods Desserts Other Sweet Things Appetizers and First Courses Meat and Poultry Fish and Seafood Hearty Soups and Stews Casseroles and Skillet Meals Side Dishes and Salads Breads and Baked Goods Desserts Other Sweet Things Appetizers and First Courses Meat and Poultry Fish and Seafood Hearty Soups and Stews Casseroles and Skillet Meals Side Dishes and Salads Breads and Baked Goods Desserts and Other Sweet Things Appetizers and First Courses Meat and Poultry Fish and Seafood Hearty Soups and Stews Casseroles and Skillet Meals Side Dishes and Salads Breads and Baked Goods Desserts and Other Sweet Things Appetizers and First Courses Meat and Poultry Fish and Seafood Hearty Soups and Stews Casseroles and Skillet Meals Side Dishes and Salads Breads and Baked Goods Desserts and Other Sweet Things Appetizers and First Courses Meat and Poultry Fish and Seafood Hearty Soups and Stews Casseroles and Skillet Meals Side Dishes and Salads Breads and Baked Goods Desserts and Other Sweet Things Appetizers and First Courses Meat and Poultry Fish and Seafood Hearty Soups and Stews Casseroles and Skillet Meals Side Dishes and Salads Breads and Baked Goods Desserts and Other Sweet Things Appetizers and First Courses Meat Poultry Fish and Seafood Hearty Soups and Stews Casseroles and Skillet Meals Side Dishes and Salads **Breads and Baked Goods** Desserts and Other Sweet Things Appetizers and First Courses Meat and Poultry Fish and Seafood Hearty Soups and Stews Casseroles and Skillet Meals Side Dishes and Salads Breads and Baked Goods Desserts and Other Sweet Things Appetizers and First Courses Meat and Poultry Fish and Seafood Hearty Soups and Stews Casseroles and Skillet Meals Side Dishes and Salads Breads and Baked Goods Desserts and Other Sweet Things Appetizers and First Courses Meat and Poultry Fish and Seafood Hearty Soups and Stews Casseroles and Skillet Meals Side Dishes and Salads Breads and Baked Goods Desserts and Other Sweet Things Appetizers and First Courses Meat and Poultry Fish and Seafood Hearty Soups and Stews Casseroles and Skillet Meals Side Dishes and Salads Breads and Baked Goods Desserts and Other Sweet Things

TAXI TRIVIA: Established in 1971, the NYC Taxi & Limousine Commission (TLC) is responsible for licensing and regulating the city's taxis and limousines.

Cabbie: **John Kadvan**
Country of Origin: Czechoslovakia

Poppy Seed Strudel

John's mother, who makes this unusual strudel often, buys her poppy seeds in an ethnic market where they are sold in bulk rather than in the little spice jars that make them very expensive. "She uses so many poppy seeds in her cooking that they never have a chance to go bad," he notes. "But she says to tell you that you can store any that you don't use in the freezer and they won't get rancid."

MAKES 6 TO 8 SERVINGS

1 cup poppy seeds

¼ cup dark raisins

¼ cup granulated sugar

½ cup sour cream (do not use low-fat)

¼ teaspoon ground cinnamon

Pastry

1 tablespoon granulated sugar

⅛ teaspoon ground cinnamon

4 tablespoons (½ stick) unsalted butter, melted

6 sheets phyllo dough (see How to Handle Phyllo Dough, page 31)

1 Preheat the oven to 350°F. Coat a baking sheet with nonstick cooking spray.

2 In a blender or mini food processor, grind the poppy seeds until they are as fine as you can get them. You may have to pulse the machine on and off several times to give the seeds a stir.

3 In a small bowl, combine the ground poppy seeds, raisins, sugar, sour cream, and cinnamon until well blended, and set aside.

4 Prepare the Pastry: In a small bowl, combine the sugar and cinnamon. Lay a clean kitchen towel on a work surface. Place 2 phyllo sheets on the towel, a long side facing you, one on top of the other. Brush with about 1 tablespoon of the butter. Sprinkle with about one-third of the sugar mixture. Top with 2 phyllo sheets and brush with another tablespoon of the butter. Sprinkle with another third of the sugar mixture. Top with the last 2 phyllo sheets and brush with another tablespoon of the butter.

5 Spoon the poppy-seed filling along the long bottom edge of the pastry closest to you, leaving a 1-inch border at the bottom and on the sides. Fold the borders in so that the filling will be securely enclosed as the pastry is rolled. Using the end of the towel to help you, roll up the strudel, but not too tightly, since the filling expands as it bakes. Place the roll on the prepared baking sheet, and brush with the remaining butter, then sprinkle with the remaining sugar mixture.

6 Bake for 25 to 30 minutes, or until golden brown. Cool completely on the baking sheet before removing to a cutting surface. To serve, cut into 6 or 8 diagonal slices.

VARIATION: Apple Strudel—Substitute 1½ cups thinly sliced apples for the poppy seeds, and add 1 teaspoon of all-purpose flour to the raisin-sugar mixture. Follow the same procedure for making the Poppy Seed Strudel.

BIG APPLE BITE: Greenwich Village mask maker and puppeteer Ralph Lee's only intention was to entertain his kids and friends when he started a Halloween parade in 1973. Little did he know that it would eventually turn into a world-renowned event, drawing over thirty thousand participants every year.

Cabbie: **Hristos Soulantzos**
Country of Origin: Greece

Other Recipes:
Greek-style Shrimp Scampi (see page 87)

Crusty Country Bread

Hristos says he can still clearly remember when he was a little boy and the aroma of this bread as it drifted through the house every Saturday, the day his mother baked. Country bread is best if eaten on the day it's baked, but will keep for a day or so after it has been cut by simply setting the loaf on the counter, cut-side down. It can also be frozen, tightly wrapped in foil, for a month or two. Unwrap and thaw at room temperature.

MAKES ONE 8-INCH ROUND LOAF

2 (¼-ounce) packages active dry yeast
2 cups warm water (105°F to 115°F)
4 cups all-purpose flour
1 cup whole wheat flour
1½ teaspoons salt
1 teaspoon sugar
2 teaspoons olive oil, plus extra for brushing
  on bread

1 In a small bowl, sprinkle the yeast over the warm water. Set aside to soften, about 5 minutes. Lightly coat an 8-inch round cake pan with nonstick cooking spray.

2 In a large bowl, whisk together the all-purpose flour, whole wheat flour, salt, and sugar until well blended. Make a well in the center of the flour and pour the yeast mixture into it. With your hands, gently mix the dry ingredients toward the center and into the yeast mixture until a stiff dough forms. Knead briefly in the bowl. Add the 2 teaspoons of olive oil, and con-tinue kneading until the oil is completely incorporated.

3 Form the dough into a ball and place in the prepared cake pan. Cover with a towel. Set aside and let rise in a warm place, out of drafts, until doubled in size, about 1 hour.

4 Meanwhile, position a rack in the center of the oven, and preheat the oven to 300°F.

5 Gently brush the risen loaf with olive oil. With the tip of a sharp knife or a single-edge razor blade, make 4 shallow slits in the top of the dough. Place the bread in the oven and immediately increase the temperature to 400°F. Bake for 35 to 40 minutes, or until the loaf is browned and sounds hollow when lightly tapped on the side. Slide the loaf onto a wire rack to cool completely to room temperature before slicing or pulling apart.

Cabbie: **Enoch Klinger**

Country of Origin: United States

Other Recipes:

Roast Beef with Cold Tomato Salad (see page 38)

Golden Corn Bread

Enoch admits that corn bread and roast beef are probably a strange combination, but it has come to be a tradition in his family and, as with many family traditions, who knows why. But he urges those who have doubts to try it.

The amount of sweetness in corn bread is definitely a personal preference. Some like the bread with no sweetness, only slightly sweet, or definitely sweet. As an accompaniment for a roast beef dinner, less or not at all sweet would probably be best. What is more important is using stone-ground, yellow cornmeal, which provides the slight crunch and golden color.

MAKES 8 SERVINGS

1 cup stone-ground yellow cornmeal

1 cup all-purpose flour

2 to 4 tablespoons sugar

1 tablespoon baking powder

1 teaspoon salt

¾ cup whole milk

3 large eggs

4 tablespoons (½ stick) butter, melted and cooled

1 Position a rack in the center of the oven. Preheat the oven to 450°F. Grease an 8 x 8-inch metal baking pan, and line the bottom with waxed paper or parchment paper. To fit the parchment or waxed paper to the size of the pan, trace around the bottom of the pan on the paper, then cut inside the trace line.

2 In a large bowl, whisk together the cornmeal, flour, sugar, baking powder, and salt until well blended. In a medium-size bowl, whisk together the milk and eggs, then whisk in the melted butter. With a spoon, stir the milk mixture into the cornmeal mixture just until blended. (There may be a few lumps, but it is important not to overmix the batter or it will become tough.) Turn the batter into the prepared pan, smoothing the top with the back of the spoon.

3 Bake until the corn bread is risen, golden brown, and firm in the center when lightly touched, 16 to 18 minutes. (Be careful not to overbake. "Better a little underdone than overdone," warns Enoch.)

4 Set the pan on a wire rack to cool for 5 minutes, then turn the bread onto the rack and carefully peel away the paper. Turn right-side up on a cutting surface, and cut into squares. Serve immediately, or cool completely. Reheat in a 350°F oven for 5 to 10 minutes before serving.

Cabbies: **Anna and Peter Egan**

Country of Origin: Ireland and the United States

Other Recipes:

Glazed Corned Beef with Vegetables (see page 41)

Irish Lamb Stew (see page 106)

Mashed Potatoes, Carrots, and Parsnips (see page 147)

Emerald Isle Trifle (see page 189)

Irish Soda Bread

"I won a baking contest for Irish soda bread with this recipe," Anna says. "We happen to love caraway seeds, and so I use them generously. You can cut back by half, if you like."

MAKES ABOUT 16 SERVINGS

4 cups all-purpose flour

½ cup granulated sugar

1 teaspoon salt

1 teaspoon baking powder

1 to 2 tablespoons caraway seeds (optional)

4 tablespoons (½ stick) cold butter, cut into pieces

1 to 2 cups dark raisins (optional)

1 large egg

1 teaspoon baking soda

1½ cups buttermilk

1 Position a rack in the center of the oven. Preheat the oven to 350°F. Grease a 2½-quart glass casserole and set aside.

2 In a large bowl, with a whisk, combine the flour, sugar, salt, baking powder, and caraway seeds, if using, until well blended. With a pastry blender or two knives used in a crisscross fashion, cut in the butter until the mixture resembles fine crumbs (this may take a few minutes). With your hands, toss in the raisins (if using).

3 In a small bowl, with a dinner fork, beat together the egg and baking soda. Stir in the buttermilk until well mixed. With the fork, stir the egg mixture into the dry ingredients just until blended. (You will eventually have to use your hands to incorporate all of the dry particles into the dough.) Do not overmix. Gather the dough together into a round that is roughly the same size as the casserole. Transfer the dough to the casserole, patting it in evenly. With the tip of a knife, cut a deep cross in the center of the top of the bread.

4 Bake for 55 to 60 minutes, or until the bread is lightly browned and sounds hollow when tapped on the top. Set the casserole on a rack and cool for 10 minutes, then turn upside down to remove the bread. Turn the bread right-side up to finish cooling on the rack.

Cabbie: **Jasbir S. Malhotra**

Country of Origin: India

"Chapati"

Middle Eastern Flat Bread

This simple, tasty bread, with no more ingredients than flour, water, sometimes oil, and salt, is a mainstay in the East Indian diet. It is served at almost every meal, and is used mostly as a "pusher" or a "scoop." *Chapati* can be purchased in Middle Eastern grocery stores, but, as Jasbir says, "It is so simple to make, why bother?"

MAKES 8 INDIVIDUAL-SIZE FLAT BREADS

1½ cups whole wheat flour
½ cup all-purpose flour
1 teaspoon salt
1 tablespoon vegetable oil
¾ cup very warm (105°F to 115°F) water
2 to 3 tablespoons butter, melted

1 In a large bowl, with a whisk, combine the whole wheat and white flours with the salt until well blended. Make a well in the center. Stir in the oil and ½ cup of the water. Gradually work in the remaining water with your hands until it is completely absorbed and the flour mixture has taken on a doughlike consistency. If the mixture seems dry, gradually add 1 or 2 tablespoons of warm water. Turn the dough out onto a lightly floured surface, and knead until it is smooth and elastic, 5 to 7 minutes. If the dough gets too sticky to knead, lightly dust your hands with flour, but do not add flour to the dough. Cover the dough with a damp towel and let rest for 30 minutes.

2 Cut the dough into 8 equal pieces. On a very lightly floured surface, roll each piece of dough into a roundish shape, 6 to 7 inches in diameter. Do not stack the rounds.

3 Lightly grease or coat with nonstick cooking spray a stovetop griddle or a large skillet, and set over medium-high heat. When the griddle is very hot, place 1 dough round on the surface, and cook for 1 minute. With a pancake turner, flip the bread over, and cook for another 30 seconds. (Use the turner to press down on the bread as it rises and puffs up, so that the *chapati* stays flat and cooks evenly.) Place the grilled bread on a baking sheet, and brush the top with butter. (After the bread has been buttered, 2 or 3 *chapatis* can be stacked together.) Keep the breads, loosely covered with foil, warm on the baking sheet in a warm (170°F) oven. Serve warm, tearing into pieces to eat.

Chapter 8 Appetizers and First Courses Meat and Poultry Fish and Seafood Hearty Soups and Stews Casseroles and Skillet Meals Side Dishes and Salads Breads and Baked Goods Desserts and Other Sweet Things Appetizers and First Courses Meat and Poultry Fish and Seafood Hearty Soups and Stews Casseroles and Skillet Meals Side Dishes and Salads Breads and Baked Goods Desserts and Other Sweet Things Appetizers and First Courses Meat and Poultry Fish and Seafood Hearty Soups and Stews Casseroles and Skillet Meals Side Dishes and Salads Breads and Baked Goods Desserts Other Sweet Things Appetizers and First Courses Meat and Poultry Fish and Seafood Hearty Soups and Stews Casseroles and Skillet Meals Side Dishes and Salads Breads and Baked Goods Desserts Other Sweet Things Appetizers and First Courses Meat and Poultry Fish and Seafood Hearty Soups and Stews Casseroles and Skillet Meals Side Dishes and Salads Breads and Baked Goods Desserts and Other Sweet Things Appetizers and First Courses Meat and Poultry Fish and Seafood Hearty Soups and Stews Casseroles and Skillet Meals Side Dishes and Salads Breads and Baked Goods Desserts and Other Sweet Things Appetizers and First Courses Meat and Poultry Fish and Seafood Hearty Soups and Stews Casseroles and Skillet Meals Side Dishes and Salads Breads and Baked Goods Desserts and Other Sweet Things Appetizers and First Courses Meat and Poultry Fish and Seafood Hearty Soups and Stews Casseroles and Skillet Meals Side Dishes and Salads Breads and Baked Goods Desserts and Other Sweet Things Appetizers and First Courses Meat and Poultry Fish and Seafood Hearty Soups and Stews Casseroles and Skillet Meals Side Dishes and Salads Breads and Baked Goods **Desserts and Other Sweet Things** Appetizers and First Courses Meat and Poultry Fish and Seafood Hearty Soups and Stews Casseroles and Skillet Meals Side Dishes and Salads Breads and Baked Goods Desserts and Other Sweet Things Appetizers and First Courses Meat and Poultry Fish and Seafood Hearty Soups and Stews Casseroles and Skillet Meals Side Dishes and Salads Breads and Baked Goods Desserts and Other Sweet Things Appetizers and First Courses Meat and Poultry Fish and Seafood Hearty Soups and Stews Casseroles and Skillet Meals Side Dishes and Salads Breads and Baked Goods Desserts and Other Sweet Things Appetizers and First Courses Meat and Poultry Fish and Seafood Hearty Soups and Stews Casseroles and Skillet Meals Side Dishes and Salads Breads and Baked Goods Desserts and Other Sweet Things Appetizers and First Courses Meat and Poultry Fish and Seafood Hearty Soups and Stews Casseroles and Skillet Meals Side Dishes and Salads Breads and Baked Goods Desserts and Other Sweet Things Appetizers and First Courses Meat and Poultry Fish and Seafood Hearty Soups and Stews Casseroles and Skillet Meals Side Dishes and Salads Breads and Baked Goods Desserts and Other Sweet Things Appetizers and First Courses Meat and Poultry Fish and Seafood Hearty Soups and Stews Casseroles Skillet Meals Side Dishes and Salads Breads and Baked Goods Desserts and Other Sweet Things

TAXI TRIVIA: According to the NYC Taxi & Limousine Commission, the average age of an NYC cab is two-and-a-half years.

Cabbie: **Ahmed Hassan**

Country of Origin: Egypt

Other recipe:

Yogurt Sauce (see page 34)

Baklava

Although baklava is considered to be a Greek culinary treasure, this world-famous triangle-cut, syrup-soaked pastry is made everywhere in the Middle East. Baklavas are all rather alike, varying by only as much as the recipes of the millions of cooks who make it. Because this pastry is so rich, and so sweet, keep the servings conservative. A small cup of strong, black Greek, Turkish, or other Middle Eastern coffee (preferably made in a long-handled, cylindrical pot called a *briki*) served with the baklava is almost mandatory, according to Ahmed.

Baklava keeps very nicely for several days at room temperature, but it's so good it usually doesn't last that long. Pistachios or walnuts can be substituted for the almonds, or use a mixture of two or three kinds of nuts ("but not peanuts," Ahmed says emphatically).

MAKES ABOUT 12 SERVINGS

½ pound, plus 4 tablespoons (2½ sticks) unsalted butter, melted

2 cups whole almonds, toasted (see Note)

1 package (1 pound) phyllo dough, thawed as the package directs and brought to room temperature (see How to Handle Phyllo Dough, page 31)

Syrup

3 cups water

1½ cups sugar

½ teaspoon vanilla extract

⅛ teaspoon lemon extract

1 Position a rack in the center of the oven. Preheat the oven to 350°F. Use some of the melted butter to brush the bottom and sides of a 13 x 9-inch metal baking pan, and set aside.

2 Place the toasted nuts in a food processor. Pulse several times until the nuts are finely chopped, but be careful not to pulverize them. (The nuts can also be very finely chopped by hand, using a sharp, heavy knife.) Turn the nuts into a bowl and set aside.

3 Remove the phyllo from the package to a work surface and smooth out the stack of sheets. With a pizza cutter or a sharp knife and a ruler, cut the stack of phyllo vertically in half to make two stacks of long rectangular sheets. Set the stacks of sheets on top of one another, keeping the dough covered. Place one sheet of phyllo on one side of the bottom of the prepared pan. The sheet will be too long for the pan, so fold one end back onto itself and brush the whole sheet with melted butter. Lay another piece of phyllo next to the first and repeat the folding process. Repeat this procedure to make 5 layers, switching the folded-back ends to the other end of the pan with each layer to keep the layers even. Brush the final sheet with butter, and sprinkle evenly with about half the nuts. Do another 5 sheets of phyllo as before, topping with the remaining nuts. Finally, do another 5 sheets of phyllo. Brush the top sheet with the remaining butter.

4 Using a pancake turner, go around all four sides of the pan, neatly tucking down the layers of dough. With a long, sharp knife, cut the layers lengthwise into thirds. Then cut into diamond shapes. Bake for 30 minutes, then raise the oven temperature to 475°F, and bake 10 minutes longer, or until golden brown.

5 While the baklava is baking, make the syrup. In a heavy, medium-size saucepan, combine the water and sugar. Bring to a boil over heat. Boil briskly for 10 minutes, or just until the syrup has taken on a little color and smells a bit like cotton candy. Remove from the heat, and stir in the vanilla and lemon extracts.

6 Remove the baklava from the oven to a wire rack. Cool for 10 minutes, then pour the warm syrup evenly over the baklava. When completely cool, cover and set aside for several hours or overnight before serving at room temperature. By that time, the syrup will be completely absorbed into the baked phyllo layers. Cover leftovers tightly and store at room temperature.

NOTE: How to Toast Nuts—Nuts take on greater flavor when they are toasted. To pan-toast nuts (whole, slivered, or chopped), place them in a cold, dry skillet large enough to hold them in one layer. Set the pan over medium heat, and cook, stirring constantly, just until the nuts begin to smell "nutty" and "toasty." (It's the aroma, more than the appearance, that tells you when the nuts are toasted.) Immediately remove from the heat, and continue to stir for a minute or so until the skillet cools.

BIG APPLE BITE: Central Park, in the middle of Manhattan, covers more territory than the entire nation of Monaco.

Cabbie: **Rocco Caputo**

Country of Origin: Italy

Other Recipe:

Chocolate-Cherry Ice Cream Truffles (see page 193)

Pizza Dolce

Rocco assured us that his grandmother's recipe for this Italian cheesecake, an Easter treat for many Italians, is very easy to make. Like most cheesecakes, it is rich, but unlike most cheesecakes, it is not terribly sweet. Serve with lightly sweetened and mashed raspberries or strawberries, if you like.

Preparation for this recipe must be started at least 8 hours or the day before serving.

MAKES 12 TO 16 SERVINGS

3 (15-ounce) containers whole-milk ricotta cheese

4 almond biscotti, broken into pieces

2 teaspoons softened butter, for greasing the baking dish

6 large eggs

1½ cups sugar

1 cup heavy cream

1 lemon, zest grated and juiced

1 teaspoon vanilla extract

1 Line a colander set in a bowl with a triple layer of dampened cheesecloth. Turn the ricotta into the colander, and refrigerate for at least 8 hours or overnight to drain.

2 In a blender or food processor, pulse the pieces of biscotti to make about 1 cup of fine crumbs, and set aside.

3 Position a rack in the center of the oven. Preheat the oven to 325°F. Grease a 13 x 9-inch glass baking dish with the butter. Sprinkle about half the biscotti crumbs in the bottom of the dish (see Note), and set aside.

4 Turn the drained ricotta into a large, wide mixing bowl. With a sturdy spoon, mix together the ricotta and eggs until well blended. Add the sugar, and mix again. Stir in the cream, lemon zest, lemon juice, and vanilla, and beat just until smooth. Pour the cheese mixture into the prepared baking dish.

5 Bake for about 45 minutes, then sprinkle evenly with the remaining biscotti crumbs. Continue to bake for another 10 to 15 minutes, or until the cheesecake begins to pull away from the sides of the baking dish and the center gives only slightly when lightly touched. (The cheesecake will have puffed up, but will settle back down as it cools.) Cool completely on a wire rack before cutting. Serve at room temperature or chilled. Store leftovers, tightly covered, in the refrigerator.

NOTE: Achieving an Even Sprinkle—"Sprinkle evenly" (crumbs, finely chopped nuts, confectioners' sugar, cocoa powder, etc.), a direction often called for in recipes, is often an imprecise procedure when done by hand. Food stylists and other kitchen professionals use this easy method: Place whatever-is-to-be-sprinkled in a sieve with an appropriate-size mesh (finest mesh for confectioners' sugar and cocoa, larger meshes for crumbs and nuts). Move the sieve over the surface to be covered, gently shaking it back and forth, and tapping the side lightly, if necessary, to release the contents evenly.

Cabbie: **Awilda Velez**

Country of Origin: Puerto Rico

Other Recipes:

Adobo Pork Roast (see page 58)

PROFILE: Awilda first came to America at the age of nineteen. She and her husband both drive cabs, alternating shifts, so that someone can always be with their son. "My son is very important to me. I just want to take care of him."
MEMORABLE FARES: During her first week on the job, a guy tried to get into her cab while four men were shooting at him. She drove off just in time.

Sweet-spiced Papaya (or Mango)

Awilda says that in her country this refreshing, healthy dessert is always served with a fresh white cheese, something the Puerto Ricans call *queso de Puna*, which is available in many Latin American markets and can vary in texture from soft to firm and crumbly. Bulgarian feta cheese, although more salty, or a log of lightly salted plain goat cheese, can be used as a stand-in. A garnish of mint sprigs, although hardly a Puerto Rican touch, is a nice flavor enhancer.

MAKES 4 TO 6 SERVINGS

2 ripe papayas (or mangoes), about 1 pound each, peeled

1 cup water

½ cup granulated sugar

6 whole cloves

4-inch cinnamon stick, broken in half

Fresh mint sprigs, for garnish (optional)

1 Cut the papayas in half lengthwise, scoop out the black seeds, peel, and slice. (If using mangoes, cut lengthwise through the unpeeled fruit on either side of the flat pit, getting as close to the pit as possible. Cut a crosshatch or tic-tac-toe pattern in the flesh of each half, but not through the skin. Holding the ends of each half in your hands, press the skin with your thumbs to turn the half inside out. Diamond-shaped, bite-size chunks of fruit will pop up from the skin, ready to be scooped off with a spoon. Cut off and dice any flesh that clings to the pit.) Place the fruit slices in a wide, shallow serving bowl, and set aside while making the syrup.

2 In a small, heavy saucepan, combine the water, sugar, cloves, and cinnamon sticks. Bring to a gentle boil, and cook until the mixture becomes slightly syrupy and is just beginning to change to a very pale golden color, 5 to 7 minutes. Remove from the heat, and discard the cloves and cinnamon sticks. Drizzle the hot syrup over the fruit, and set aside to cool. To serve chilled, cover, and refrigerate for 1 or 2 hours.

4 Arrange the cooled or chilled fruit on dessert plates. Garnish with mint sprigs, if using, and serve with cheese (see headnote).

TAXI TRIVIA: There are two kinds of taxi drivers: **1.** The meticulous driver knows when the ships are in, when the theaters let out, when the planes arrive at the airports, and where all the sporting events are. **2.** The casual driver just drives.

Cabbie: **Rivka Moskovich**

Country of Origin: Israel

Other Recipes:

Roasted Eggplant Salad (see page 16)

Chicken Baked with Oranges (see page 64)

Meat-and-Tomato-Stuffed Eggplant (see page 121)

Glazed Oranges with Mint Syrup

"I especially like this dessert because it has absolutely no fat and is very refreshing—especially after a rich meal," says Rivka. "One of my girlfriends always serves it for brunch parties, and she suggested that I should mention this."

MAKES 6 SERVINGS

½ cup fresh mint leaves

4 navel oranges

2 cups sugar

2 cups water

2-inch cinnamon stick, broken in half

4 whole cloves

Tiny mint sprigs, for garnish

1 Briefly roll the fresh mint leaves between the palms of your hands to help extract the natural oils, and set aside.

2 Peel the oranges, separating each orange into sections and removing as much of the little strings and pith netting as possible without exposing the actual flesh. Reserve a 3-inch piece of the peel, scraping away all of the pith from the underside.

3 In a Dutch oven or other large, heavy saucepan, combine the sugar, water, cinnamon sticks, cloves, rolled mint leaves, and reserved orange peel, and bring to a boil over high heat. Boil hard until the mixture is slightly syrupy, about 10 minutes. Remove from the heat, then remove and discard the spices and mint leaves with a slotted spoon. Lower the orange sections into the hot syrup, turning them as you do so. Return the pan to the heat and boil gently for 5 minutes, turning the orange sections a few times.

4 With the slotted spoon, remove the sections to a serving bowl. (A glass bowl is an especially attractive way to serve this.) Continue to boil the syrup for 5 minutes, then remove from the heat and set aside to cool slightly. Pour the syrup over the oranges. Cover, and refrigerate for several hours before serving, turning the orange sections in the syrup every now and then.

5 When ready to serve, spoon the orange sections into dessert bowls, along with some of the syrup. Garnish with tiny mint sprigs.

Cabbie: **Ismail Akbal**

Country of Origin: Turkey

Other Recipes:

Sebze Gorbas: Turkish Vegetable Soup (see page 93)

Ladies' Navels

"When most people think of Middle Eastern pastries, they think of baklava, but we have dozens of other syrup-soaked pastries that are usually served a couple of hours after dinner along with a cup of strong Turkish coffee," says Ismail. "But I especially like these. It's the hole in the center of these sweet, puffy pastries that accounts for their name," Ismail tells us.

The secret to these small, syrup-soaked pastries is to start the frying process in medium-hot oil. This allows the interior to cook thoroughly before the outside turns an appetizingly golden brown.

MAKES ABOUT 18 PASTRIES

Syrup

1 cup sugar

1 cup water

1 tablespoon freshly squeezed lemon juice

3 or 4 whole cloves

1-inch cinnamon stick

Pastries

1 cup water

3 tablespoons unsalted butter

¼ teaspoon salt

1¼ cups all-purpose flour

2 large eggs, at room temperature

2 cups canola or regular olive oil, for frying

Lightly sweetened whipped cream or chopped pistachio nuts, for serving (optional)

1 Prepare the Syrup: In a small, heavy saucepan, combine the sugar, water, lemon juice, cloves, and cinnamon stick. Bring to a boil over high heat. Reduce the heat slightly, and simmer briskly, without stirring, just until the syrup is very slightly thickened, 10 to 12 minutes. (If the syrup is too thick, it will not soak into the pastries.) Remove from the heat and set aside. (Just before using, remove the cloves and cinnamon stick and discard.)

2 Prepare the Pastries: In a medium-size saucepan, combine the water, butter, and salt, and bring to a boil over high heat. With a heavy spoon, stir in the flour all at once. Remove from the heat, and beat vigorously until the dough is smooth and pulls away from the side of the pan. Add the eggs, one at a time, beating hard after each addition, until the dough is smooth and shiny.

3 Rub a little oil on the palms of your hands to keep the dough from sticking. Break off pieces of dough about the size of walnuts. Roll each piece into a disk measuring about 2 inches in diameter. Stick a finger through the center to make "doughnuts."

4 Meanwhile, in a deep, heavy, medium-size saucepan, heat about 3 inches of oil to a temperature of 275°F on a deep-fry thermometer. Carefully drop in a few of the pastries, leaving enough space for expansion. Allow the temperature of the oil to keep rising to 350°F, at which point the pastries should be pale golden on the outside and cooked through inside. Remove with a slotted spoon to paper towels to drain briefly, then transfer to a small, deep platter. Drizzle a little of the syrup over the warm pastries.

5 Reduce the oil heat to 275°F, then continue the frying process as before until all the pastries are fried. As each batch of pastries is transferred to the platter, drizzle lightly with the syrup. The pastries should only be soaked with the syrup, not swimming in it. Serve within a day, with a small spoonful of whipped cream in the centers, if desired, or sprinkled with chopped pistachios, or both.

BIG APPLE BITE: According to the New York Visitors Bureau, The Big Apple welcomes more than thirty-eight million visitors annually. Of these, about six-and-a-half million are from foreign countries, making New York City truly the crossroads of the world.

Cabbie: **S.K. Rastogi**
Country of Origin: India

"Kheer"

Indian Milk-and-Rice Pudding

"I understand that Americans, too, have rice pudding," says this polite driver. He tells us that he came to New York from another "New," New Delhi, several years ago and has been driving a cab since. "Our version of the pudding is similar, except that we use aromatic rice and nuts, but I think you will like it." It is the pudding, he adds, that he has been eating since he was a boy, and he was anxious to share his mother's recipe for this classic Indian dessert with us. In India, *kheer* is almost always served cold, but can also be eaten while it is still warm from the stove, or rewarmed in a microwave oven.

The rose water called for in this recipe is a highly flavored and perfumed water distilled from fresh rose petals. It should not be confused with rose essence, which is much stronger. Rose water is used sparingly to flavor desserts and other confections. You can find it in Middle Eastern markets, and gourmet foodstores.

MAKES ABOUT 5 CUPS;

10 SERVINGS

---

2 quarts whole milk
⅓ cup basmati rice
¾ cup sugar
½ cup finely chopped unsalted cashew nuts
Ground cinnamon, for garnish
¼ teaspoon ground cardamom
1 teaspoon rose water.

1 In a large, heavy saucepan, bring the milk to a boil over high heat, stirring constantly to help prevent a skin from forming on the top. Reduce the heat until the milk simmers, and continue to cook, stirring occasionally and removing the skin as it forms, for about 30 minutes, until the milk is reduced to about 2 cups.

2 Stir in the rice, and continue to cook for about 20 minutes, or until the rice is very soft and starting to disintegrate. Stir in the sugar and nuts. Continue to cook, stirring almost constantly, for about 15 minutes, or until the pudding thickly coats a spoon. Remove from the heat, and stir in the cardamom and rose water until well blended. Serve warm or chilled, sprinkled with cinnamon.

Cabbie: **Mohammed Mouaki**

Country of Origin: Algeria

"Mesouf"

Special Sweet Couscous for Holidays

"During the month of Ramadan, the Muslims fast, eating just one meal a day right after sunset," Mohammed tells us. "This special couscous dish is eaten one hour before sunrise with a glass of milk. It provides just enough energy to last until the daily meal, which is more than twelve hours away."

The orange-blossom water called for in this recipe, a highly flavored and perfumed water distilled from orange blossoms, is used sparingly in many Middle Eastern desserts. It is fairly easy to find in Middle Eastern foodstores and better supermarkets.

A very American touch we liked for this dessert is the addition of a little warm cream (or whipped cream) to be added to each diner's taste.

MAKES ABOUT 6 CUPS;

6 TO 8 SERVINGS

1 (10-ounce) box plain couscous

2 tablespoons unsalted butter

1 cup regular sour cream

1 cup plain low-fat yogurt

1 (5-ounce) can evaporated (not condensed) milk

½ cup whole milk

¼ cup sugar

1 teaspoon vanilla extract

1 teaspoon orange-blossom water

⅛ teaspoon freshly grated nutmeg

⅓ cup slivered blanched almonds, toasted (see Note, page 175)

1 Prepare the entire box of couscous as the package directs, using water as the cooking liquid and omitting the oil.

2 In a small saucepan, melt the butter until bubbly, but not starting to brown. Fluff the hot couscous, breaking up any lumps, with a dinner fork. Stir in the hot butter until well blended. Turn the couscous into a large bowl.

3 Meanwhile, in a medium-size bowl, whisk together the sour cream, yogurt, evaporated milk, whole milk, sugar, vanilla, orange water, and nutmeg. Pour over the couscous, and stir until well blended.

4 Cover, and refrigerate for about 30 minutes. Sprinkle with the toasted almonds just before serving.

Cabbie: **Cesar Quinones**
Country of Origin: Colombia

"Ponke Colombiano"

Colombian Black Cake

"In Colombia this is a party cake," says Cesar. "It takes a lot of work to make it, but it's worth it."

The recipe that Cesar gave us called for *panela*, which is a rock-hard chunk of raw sugar. Regular dark brown sugar is easier to find and tastes very much the same. The translation for Spanish *aguardiente* is "burned water." The liqueur of roughly the same name is a generic term for several low-quality spirits. The South American version of *aguardiente* (*agua diente*) is distilled from sugar cane (sometimes flavored with anise) and is extremely sweet. *Agua diente* is difficult to find in the United States, so we substituted orange-flavored liqueur, which seemed to harmonize well with the brown sugar and fruity flavors in the cake.

For the best flavor, plan to make this cake about four days before you wish to serve it.

MAKES 8 TO 12 SERVINGS

2 cups all-purpose flour

¾ cup diced, dried mixed fruit

½ cup baking raisins

1½ sticks unsalted butter, at room temperature

1 cup packed dark brown sugar

1 cup granulated sugar

5 large eggs, at room temperature

Grated zest of 2 limes

1½ teaspoons freshly grated nutmeg

½ teaspoon salt

2 tablespoons dark rum

2 tablespoons *agua diente* or orange liqueur (see headnote)

2 tablespoons sweet vermouth or port, plus more for drizzling on the cake as it ages

1½ teaspoons vanilla extract

Lightly sweetened whipped cream (optional)

1 Position a rack in the lower third of the oven. Preheat the oven to 325°F. Grease and flour a fluted tube (Bundt) pan and set aside.

2 In a small bowl, toss 1 tablespoon of the flour with the diced fruit and raisins, and set aside.

3 In a large bowl, with an electric mixer at medium-high speed, beat together the butter, brown sugar, and granulated sugar until light and creamy, about 2 minutes. Beat in the eggs, one at a time, beating well after each addition. Beat in the lime zest until well blended.

4 In a medium-size bowl, whisk the nutmeg and salt into the remaining flour until well blended. In a small bowl, combine the rum, liqueur, vermouth, and vanilla. With the electric mixer on low speed, add the flour mixture to the butter mixture in three parts, alternating with the rum mixture in two parts, beating until smooth and scraping the side of the bowl as necessary. Beat 1 minute longer at medium speed. With a large spoon, fold in the floured fruit mixture until well distributed throughout the batter.

5 Turn the batter into the prepared pan. Bake for about 1 hour and 15 minutes, or until a wooden toothpick or cake tester inserted into the center of the cake comes out clean. Remove from the oven to a wire rack, and let cool in the pan for 15 minutes. Loosen with a knife, if necessary, then turn out onto the rack to cool completely. Set on a cake plate, and cover with a cake cover or a large bowl.

6 Each day before serving, uncover, and drizzle a small amount of vermouth over the cake to keep it moist. To serve, cut the cake into thin slices, and top each slice with whipped cream, if you like.

BIG APPLE BITE: The Brooklyn Dodgers, formerly the Brooklyn Trolley Dodgers, got their name because of the active, and often dangerous, trolley system that ran through the borough. Eventually, the team was transferred to Los Angeles, where the trolley system was already inactive.

Cabbie: **Luis Artchabala**

Country of Origin: Ecuador

Other Recipes:

Seco de Pollo: Saffron-flavored Chicken and Vegetables (see page 104)

Fried Yuca with Pickled Onion Rings (see page 155)

"Cassata"

Sicilian Special-occasion Pound Cake

Luis told us that this recipe comes from "my Italian neighbor-lady down the street." One day she caught a ride with Luis from Queens to Manhattan, and while they were stuck in morning traffic she gave him the recipe for this famous Sicilian cake, one of the few things, she says, that her mother was able to bring to the United States from the old country. This Italian lady undoubtedly makes her own pound cake, and so can you, if you like, although a good fresh or frozen pound cake does make things go considerably faster.

Preparation for this recipe must be started at least 24 hours before serving.

MAKES 12 TO 18 SERVINGS

1 (16-ounce) purchased fresh or frozen pound cake

6 tablespoons of orange- or anise-flavored liqueur

1 (15-ounce) container whole-milk ricotta cheese

2 tablespoons granulated sugar

2 cups (1 pint) heavy cream

½ cup semisweet miniature chocolate morsels, plus 1 tablespoon, for garnish

⅓ cup coarsely chopped mixed candied fruit, plus 1 tablespoon, for garnish

⅓ cup confectioners' sugar

2 tablespoons cocoa powder

2 tablespoons chopped pistachio nuts, for garnish

1 With a serrated knife, trim the ends off the pound cake and level the top. Cut the cake horizontally into 3 even layers. Brush the cut side of each cake layer with 4 tablespoons of the liqueur. Place the bottom layer of the cake on a serving plate, cutside up.

2 In a large bowl, with an electric mixer on medium speed, beat the ricotta cheese and granulated sugar until smooth and light. Beat in ¼ cup of the cream and the remaining 2 tablespoons of liqueur until fluffy. With a large spoon, fold in ½ cup of the chocolate morsels and ⅓ cup of the candied fruit until evenly distributed throughout the cheese mixture.

3 Generously spread the bottom layer of cake with about half of the ricotta mixture. Set the middle layer on top of the first, and spread with the remaining ricotta mixture. Set the top layer of cake in place. Cover with plastic wrap or aluminum foil, and refrigerate for 24 hours or up to 2 days before serving.

4 Shortly before serving, whip the remaining 1¾ cups of cream until it mounds, then beat in the confectioners' sugar and cocoa until stiff peaks form when the beaters are lifted. Remove the cake from the refrigerator, and frost the top with some of the whipped cream. Sprinkle with the reserved 1 tablespoon of candied fruit, the chocolate morsels, and the pistachios.

5 To serve, with a serrated knife, cut the cake into thin slices and serve with the remaining whipped cream.

BIG APPLE BITE: The New York City Marathon was first run in Central Park by 127 runners who completed the 26.2-mile race by running loops around and around the park. Now, more than thirty thousand runners compete, running a course through the city's five boroughs.

Cabbie: **Marleny Rubio**
Country of Origin: Peru

"Crema Volteada"

Upside-down Cream

"This is a dessert that we eat a lot in Peru," Marleny tells us. "It's sort of a combination of Spanish flan and French crème caramel, but is much easier to make than either one of them."

MAKES 12 SERVINGS

1 cup sugar

1 cup water

8 large eggs

1 (14-ounce) can sweetened
   condensed milk

1 (12-ounce) can evaporated milk

1 teaspoon shredded lemon zest

Freshly grated nutmeg

1 Position a rack in the center of the oven. Preheat the oven to 350°F. Have ready an 8-cup soufflé dish or other deep baking dish.

2 In a heavy, medium-size saucepan over high heat, combine the sugar and water, and bring to a boil. Boil briskly until the mixture turns a golden amber color, about 10 minutes. (Watch carefully, especially after the syrup starts to color, since it darkens and burns rapidly after this point.) Immediately pour the syrup into the soufflé dish, tilting the dish so that the syrup completely covers the bottom. Set aside while making the custard.

3 In the container of an electric blender, place 4 of the eggs, about half the can of condensed milk, and about half the can of evaporated milk. Add half the lemon zest and a big pinch of nutmeg, and blend for about 1 minute until fluffy. Pour into the prepared soufflé dish. Repeat this procedure with the remaining eggs, condensed milk, evaporated milk, lemon zest, and nutmeg. Pour into the soufflé dish.

4 Set the soufflé dish in a larger baking pan or roasting pan, then set the pan in the oven. Pour boiling into the baking pan until it comes halfway up the side of the soufflé dish. Bake for 35 to 40 minutes, or until a knife inserted in the center of the custard comes out clean. Remove from the oven and set on a wire rack to cool. The custard can be served slightly warm, at room temperature, or chilled. If serving chilled, cover, and refrigerate for several hours.

5 To serve, run a knife around the edge of the custard, then invert into a wide, shallow bowl or rimmed serving dish. The custard can also be served directly from the soufflé dish, spooning down deep into the dish so that each serving is sure to include some of the caramel.

Cabbies: **Anna and Peter Egan**

Country of Origin: Ireland and the United States

Other Recipes:

Glazed Corned Beef with Vegetables (see page 41)

Irish Lamb Stew (see page 106)

Mashed Potatoes, Carrots, and Parsnips (see page 147)

Irish Soda Bread (see page 170)

Emerald Isle Trifle

This Irish-style trifle is Peter's specialty. He says that things work out perfectly if the cream is whipped and refrigerated, and the cake and fruit are mixed together just before dinner. While after-dinner coffee is brewing, add the whipped cream and serve immediately.

MAKES 6 SERVINGS

Purchased sponge cake (about 8 ounces)

½ cup Irish liqueur (such as Irish Mist) or dry sherry

½ cup orange marmalade

3 tablespoons water

2 to 3 cups mixed fruit, such as sliced bananas, orange sections, blueberries, raspberries, blackberries, and sliced strawberries

1 cup (½ pint) heavy cream

3 to 4 tablespoons confectioners' sugar

1 Cut the sponge cake into large bite-size pieces and place in a glass serving bowl. Drizzle the liqueur evenly over the cake.

2 In a small saucepan, mix the marmalade with the water. Cook over medium heat, stirring, until the mixture is very hot and smooth. Set aside to cool slightly.

3 Place the fruit in a large bowl, and toss until well mixed. Pour the slightly cooled marmalade mixture over the fruit, and toss until the fruit is evenly coated. Spoon the fruit mixture over the liqueur-soaked cake. Set aside for about 30 minutes.

4 In a cold, large bowl with cold beaters, whip the cream until soft peaks form when the beaters are lifted. Beat in the confectioners' sugar until stiff peaks form.

5 Just before serving, cover the fruit topping with the whipped cream. To serve, dig down deep into the bowl so that each serving contains cake, fruit, and whipped cream.

Cabbie: **Steven Chan**

Country of Origin: Hong Kong

Other Recipes:

Chinese Spareribs (see page 32)

Chinese Almond Cookies
with Chinese Tea

"When I worked at a Chinese restaurant," recalls Steven, "we made many, many of these cookies every day. About half of them we packed in small, waxed-paper bags for take-out orders. They were very popular. This recipe is the way I make the cookies at home, which uses lard, the preferred Chinese ingredient. If you like, you can use solid shortening, but not butter or oil."

MAKES 12 COOKIES

⅓ cup chopped blanched almonds

½ cup all-purpose flour

5 tablespoons cold lard or solid white vegetable
    shortening

¼ cup sugar

1 large egg yolk

12 blanched or natural whole almonds,
    for decoration

1 large egg, well beaten, for glaze

Chinese Tea (recipe follows), for serving

1 Position a rack in the center of the oven. Preheat the oven to 350°F. Lightly grease a large baking sheet and set aside.

2 In a mini food processor or blender, process the chopped almonds with 2 tablespoons of the flour until very finely ground. In a medium-size bowl, with an electric mixer at low speed, beat the lard with the sugar, egg yolk, and almond mixture just until the mixture comes together. Increase the speed to medium, and beat until well blended. With the mixer at low speed, beat in the remaining flour until the dough cleans the side and bottom of the bowl. Wrap the dough in waxed paper, and refrigerate for 15 minutes to chill slightly.

3 On a lightly floured surface, roll the dough to a ¼-inch thickness. With a 2-inch round cutter, cut out as many cookies as possible. Reroll the scraps and cut again to make a total of 12 cookies. Transfer the cookies to the prepared baking sheet, spacing them about 2 inches apart. Press a whole almond into the center of each cookie, then brush the tops with the beaten egg.

4 Bake for about 16 minutes, reversing the baking sheet from front to back halfway through the baking time, until the cookies are pale gold. Remove from the oven and cool the sheet on a wire rack for about 10 minutes, or just until the cookies are firm. With a wide pancake turner, transfer the cookies to the rack to cool completely. Store in a tightly covered container. Serve with Chinese Tea.

Chinese Tea

According to expert Steven, it's crucial when making Chinese tea that the water be boiling when it is added to the tea leaves in the teapot. Otherwise, all the leaves will not sink to the bottom of the pot and the tea will have a bitter taste.

MAKES 8 SERVINGS

2 tablespoons black tea leaves,
  or 1¼ teaspoons green tea leaves
6 cups bottled spring water

1 Rinse the inside of a china (porcelain) teapot with plain boiling water. Drain well, then add the tea leaves.

2 Meanwhile, bring the bottled water to a rolling boil. Immediately pour the boiling water into the teapot. (At this point the tea leaves will rise to the surface and then gradually sink back to the bottom.) Cover, and let steep for 3 to 5 minutes, or until the tea is the strength you like it—typically not too strong when served in Chinese homes.

BIG APPLE BITE: The Great Fire of 1835 lasted three days and destroyed most of Lower Manhattan. The blaze engulfed seventeen city blocks and seven hundred buildings.

Cabbie: **Hakim Anes**

Country of Origin: Algeria

Other Recipes:

Algerian-style Couscous with Lamb and Little Glazed Onions (see page 107)

Sesame-Orange Sliced Cookies

"Sesame seeds can be very expensive when you buy them in little jars," says Hakim. "I get mine at Middle Eastern stores where they are sold in bulk" (see Note).

Sesame seeds become rancid rather quickly when they are stored at room temperature. To keep them almost indefinitely, seal in an air-tight plastic bag and store in the freezer. They won't become a solid mass, so you can measure out just the quantity you want the next time you need them.

MAKES ABOUT 36 COOKIES

1 cup sesame seeds

1⅔ cups all-purpose flour

2 teaspoons baking powder

6 tablespoons unsalted butter, at room temperature

½ cup packed light brown sugar

1 large egg, lightly beaten

½ teaspoon vanilla extract

2 teaspoons grated orange zest

1 Scatter the sesame seeds in a large skillet set over medium heat. Stir the seeds constantly until they are lightly browned and very aromatic. Remove the skillet from the heat, and continue stirring until cool. In a small bowl, whisk together the flour, baking powder, and sesame seeds until well blended, and set aside.

2 In a medium-size bowl, with an electric mixer at medium-high speed, beat together the butter and brown sugar until creamy, about 3 minutes. Beat in the egg, vanilla, and orange zest until well blended. With the mixer at low speed, gradually add the flour mixture, mixing just until blended.

3 Turn the dough out onto a lightly floured surface and knead for a minute or two. If the dough seems dry, gradually knead in a little water. If it seems sticky, knead in a little more flour. With your hands, shape the dough into a 9-inch-long log. Wrap the dough log in plastic wrap, and refrigerate until very firm, about 4 hours or overnight.

4 When ready to bake, position two racks to divide the oven into thirds. Preheat the oven to 350°F. Lightly grease 2 baking sheets.

5 Unwrap the dough log, and place it on a cutting surface. With a long, sharp knife, cut the cylinder into ¼-inch slices. Arrange the slices on the prepared baking sheets, spacing them about 1 inch apart.

6 Bake for 12 to 15 minutes, or until a light golden color, reversing the baking sheets on the racks and from front to back once during baking. With a pancake turner, immediately transfer the cookies to wire racks to cool completely. Store in a tightly covered container.

NOTE: Kalustyan's in New York City (123 Lexington Avenue between 28th and 29th Streets) is an indispensable source for Middle Eastern and Indian groceries. Its shelves are chock full of exotic foods, bags of spices sold in bulk, and perhaps the largest variety of chutneys and curry powders you'll ever encounter. If you live outside the New York metropolitan area, try visiting their web site at www.kalustyans.com.

Cabbie: **Rocco Caputo**

Country of Origin: Italy

Other Recipes:

Pizza Dolce (see page 176)

Chocolate-Cherry Ice Cream Truffles

"This is a recipe from my grandmother," Rocco says. "She made it specially for us kids, and she used lots of cherries because we liked them so much. I still use more cherries than I should."

MAKES 4 TO 6 SERVINGS

1 pint rich chocolate ice cream
¼ cup chopped candied cherries or dried Bing cherries (more or less, depending on how much you like cherries)
⅓ to ½ cup grated semisweet chocolate (about 2 ounces)

1 Place the ice cream in the refrigerator until it is slightly softened. (Depending on how solidly frozen the ice cream is, this can take up to 45 minutes.) Turn the ice cream into a large metal bowl, and chop it up with the side of a large metal spoon. Stir in the cherries until they are well distributed throughout the ice cream. Place the bowl in the freezer to harden slightly. Cover a small baking sheet with foil and set aside.

2 Sprinkle the grated chocolate in a pie plate or other shallow rimmed dish. Push the ice cream around in the bowl, dividing it into 4 or 6 portions. Working quickly, with your hands, shape into 4 or 6 balls. As each ball is formed, roll it in the grated chocolate until well coated, then set it on the prepared baking sheet. When all the balls have been coated, freeze, uncovered, until ready to serve.

Index